MIND PUZZLES™

Build Brain Power in Minutes a Day

Publications International, Ltd.

Julie K. Cohen is a puzzle developer, puzzle consultant, author, and freelance writer. She has published numerous math puzzle books, and her puzzles for children and adults appear in national magazines, websites, puzzle books, cellular phone games, and DVDs. To learn more about Cohen, visit her website, http://www.JulieKCohen.com.

Amy Reynaldo, the author of *How to Conquer the New York Times Crossword Puzzle,* created the first crossword blog (Diary of a Crossword Fiend) and reviews 1,500 crosswords a year. She is a top-10 finisher at the American Crossword Puzzle Tournament.

Puzzle Constructors: Michael Adams, Cihan Altay, Helem An, Chris Bolton, George Bredehorn, Susan Brown, Jim Bumgardner, Myles Callum, Clarity Media, Barry Clarke, William Cobb, Gino Collins, Conceptis Puzzles, Don Cook, Josie Faulkner, Adrian Fisher, Holli Fort, Erich Friedman, The Grabarchuk Family, Ray Hamel, Vegard Hanssen, Luke Haward, Tyler Hinman, Marilynn Huret, Matt Jones, Steve Karp, Marc Lebel, Lawrence May, Kate Mepham, David Millar, Elsa Neal, Alan Olschwang, Stephen Ryder, Gianni Sarcone, Pete Sarjeant, Fraser Simpson, Predrag Stanojevic, Startdl Puzzles, Terry Stickels, Samuel Stoddard, Howard Tomlinson, Jen Torche, Wayne Robert Williams, Alex Willmore

Puzzle Consultants: Adam Cohen, Julie K. Cohen, Shawn Kennedy, Amy Reynaldo

Illustrators: Helem An, Elizabeth Gerber, Robin Humer, Shavan R. Spears, Jen Torche

Introduction: Holli Fort

Mind Puzzles is a trademark of Publications International, Ltd.

Louis Weber, CEO
Publications International, Ltd.
7373 North Cicero Avenue
Lincolnwood, Illinois 60712

ISBN-13: 978-1-4508-1419-5
ISBN-10: 1-4508-1419-0

Manufactured in China.

8 7 6 5 4 3 2 1

IT'S EASY TO KEEP YOUR HEAD IN THE GAME!

You don't have to be a code-cracking super sleuth to get a lot out of these puzzles. *Mind Puzzles*™ offers a way for you to continually challenge your mental reserves and literally put your mind to the test. With a wide variety of puzzle types and difficulty levels to choose from, there is sure to be something that will pique your curiosity and have you doing puzzles hand over fist.

We've chosen the puzzles in this volume for maximum interest. Mixing and matching puzzles is key to ensuring that your brain stays sharp and focused. After all, you know that exercise is great for your body, so consider how beneficial this mental exercise is for your brain, keeping your synapses firing and your creative thought processes moving along. And just like variety is important in a physical workout, variety is an essential factor in keeping your whole mind fit as well.

In this volume, there are plenty of traditional puzzles, like crosswords, word searches, mazes, and cryptograms—after all, they don't get to be "classics" unless they stand up to the test of time! But we've also gotten a leg up with plenty of new puzzle styles, some of which will seem familiar, while others—like Starstruck, for example—

may be something you've never seen before. Take a look below at some of the different types of puzzles you'll find in this book.

Word Puzzles

Sharpening your language skills is fun, and it can also serve you in a number of ways throughout your daily life. Many of these puzzles are familiar classics, but we also offer up a few twists and turns along the way. Some great examples of our word puzzles include:

- Anagrams
- Codewords
- Crosswords
- Tanglewords (seen below)
- Word Searches

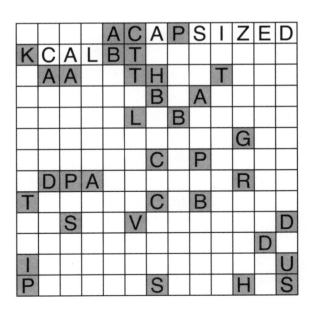

Math Puzzles

If you're worried that our math puzzles will force you to solve complicated equations, don't be. These puzzles, while challenging, are also totally within the realm of solvability, and there's nothing more complicated than a bit of multiplication, which will keep you from letting those math skills get rusty. Take a look at a sample of the puzzles in this category:

• Calcu-doku
• Number Crosswords
• Word Sums
• Sum Fun (seen below)

2	8	1	6	6	5	1	6
2	8	5	3	2	6	9	9
3	5	3	6	5	1	5	5
4	4	4	9	3	1	2	5
8	1	7	6	4	1	5	6
2	1	3	7	9	2	6	8
7	4	6	2	3	5	1	4
8	2	7	3	3	9	3	7

Visual Puzzles

Always thought you were more of a "visual learner"? Well, fear not, we've included plenty of puzzles for you! These aren't just puzzles; they're miniature works of art that will test your ability to find hidden pathways and objects and give you an opportunity to hone your memory skills, which will come in handy everywhere from the living room to the boardroom. Here are some of the different visual puzzles you'll find in each level:

• Hidden Objects
• Mazes
• Memory Puzzles
• Perspective Puzzles

Logic Puzzles

Think you've got it all figured out? Our logic puzzles may surprise you with their ability to stump even the most logical among us. You'll have to put all your reasoning skills to use to deduce the solutions to these puzzles. One of the more popular puzzles in this category is the deceptively simple sudoku, but there are plenty of others to choose from, including:

• Hitori
• Logidoku
• Water Tanks (seen on the next page)
• SquarO

We've included a range of both puzzles and difficulty levels (designated by gears, one gear being the easiest, three gears the most difficult) to offer you a broad base to choose from. To keep yourself and your puzzle-cracking skills sharp, it's a great plan to choose a variety of different puzzles to do each day. You'll expose your mind to different challenges and learn new things—one of which might even be that you love a puzzle type that you had

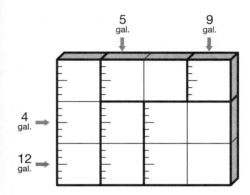

previously thought wasn't interesting: Give them all a try, and as you get better and better at solving them, increase the challenge simply by moving up a gear. Check out the index to see the cognitive functions worked by each puzzle.

Since *Mind Puzzles*™ offers such a wide variety of puzzles to choose from, it would be difficult to list hints and tips for them all. However, we can offer a few words of wisdom that can be universally applied.

- Start with the easiest part and work your way through from there. This can mean doing the fill-in-the blank clues for crosswords, finding the longest words in the word search, and filling in any numbers in a sudoku puzzle that are immediately apparent.
- Try not to overthink things. (Hint: If you think you need a complicated formula to solve a puzzle, you are definitely overthinking it.)
- Look for repeating patterns and cross-references that can give you the last bit of knowledge you need to bring the solution into focus.
- Try working backward. It's a technique that's particularly effective with mazes, but can also be applied to some language puzzles. Getting a different perspective is helpful.
- If all else fails, move on to a different puzzle and come back. You may find that your brain has worked out the problem for you in the meantime!

It doesn't take a lot of time to keep you at the top of your mental game—the key is to challenge yourself for a little while each day. Plus, since these puzzles are in such a portable format, you don't have to keep your nose to the grindstone all the time. It's easy to fit in a puzzle or two wherever you are and whatever you're doing during the day, from your morning coffee break to your midnight snack, and everywhere in between. Once you start, you'll find that these *Mind Puzzles*™ are so addicting and fun, you'll be doing them all the time!

Remember that above all else, working puzzles has the dual benefits of being fun and good for you—what else can you really say that about? Working these entertaining and engrossing puzzles can help you improve your memory and sharpen your mental skills and problem solving abilities, plus you'll learn plenty of fun facts along the way! With *Mind Puzzles*™, it turns out that playing games can reap some serious rewards.

CHAIN GRID FILL

To complete this puzzle, place the words into the chains in this grid. Words will run across, down, and diagonally around each chain. When the grid is complete, each column will contain one of the following words: American, downtown, hardware, lemons, nudity, parrot, Portland, radius, Rockwell, silver, slight. We've filled in one word to get you started.

(Grid with handwritten entries)

1. NOW, ~~RID~~, ~~SAY~~, ~~TWO~~, ~~VAN~~, ~~WAR~~, ~~WIT~~

2. ~~HARE~~, ~~REEL~~, ~~RICE~~, SNOT, ~~SOLO~~

3. ~~SOLID~~

OPPOSITES

Use the letters below to fill in the boxes and reveal the 2 related words. Connected boxes share the same letter.

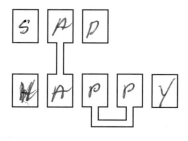

ADHPSY

Answers on page 166.

In the addition problem below, each letter represents a number between 0 and 9. Decipher the letters to reach a correct numerical conclusion.

```
    C A R
    C A R
    C A R
  + C A R
  ─────────
  R A I L
```

FRAME GAMES™

Can you "read" the phrase below?

Answers on page 166.

SPY FLY

As an international spy, your mission is to travel from your headquarters at Seth Castle to your safe house at Faro. To disguise your trail, you must stop once—and only once—at each airport. See if you can find the cheapest route for your trip. Less than $290 would make you a Steady Sleuth; less than $280, a Cool Operator; less than $270, a Crafty Agent. If you can make it on $250, then you're a Super Spy!

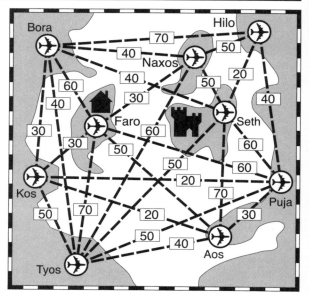

KLUMP

Shade in some of the numbers so the remaining connected sets of numbers match the following sums:

3, 5, 9, 12, 16, 24

A solitary number (not connected to any other) can represent one or more of these sums.

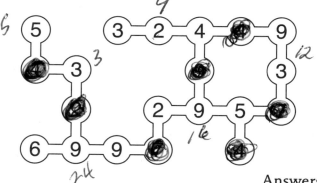

Answers on pages 166–167.

SQUARO

Shade in circles around each square as indicated by the numbers. For example, a square with a number 3 in it will have 3 of the 4 connected circles shaded in.

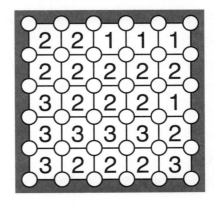

FUTOSHIKI

Place the numbers 1 through 6 in each row and column. Numbers do not repeat in any row or column. Inequality restraints (less-than and greater-than symbols) must be met when placing numbers.

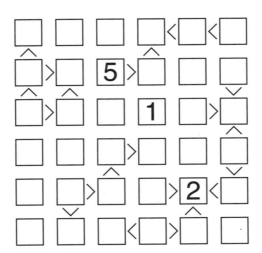

Answers on page 167.

XOXO

Place an X or an O inside each empty cell of the grid so that there appears no row, column, or diagonal with 4 consecutive cells with the same letter.

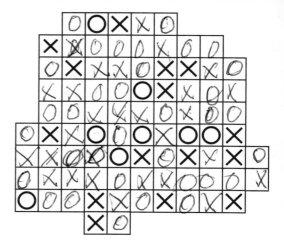

BLACK DIAMONDS

Place the numbers 1 through 4 in the cells of each of the squares below. There's a catch though: Overlapping squares must add up to the number given in each of the black diamonds.

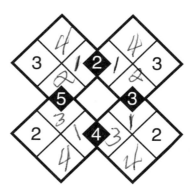

Answers on page 167.

NUMBER CROSS

Use each of the numbers listed here to complete this clue-less crossword grid. The puzzle has only one solution.

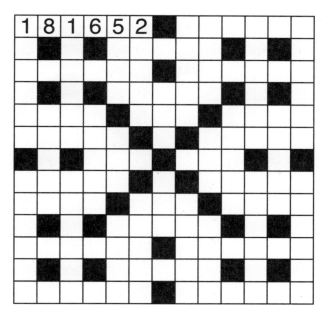

3 Figures	3040	29722	151425
104	3401	30504	172413
108	5122	30718	213022
115	5328	30843	287183
119	5888	39205	311403
224		42184	312235
248	**5 Figures**	43940	322344
323	10330	44143	401767
447	11537	52882	483000
	13198		486315
4 Figures	20238	**6 Figures**	502652
1332	23271	113735	588162
2655	27108	135192	
2888	29325	145143	

Answer on page 168.

17

ACROSTIC

Solve the clues below, and then place the letters in their corresponding spots in the grid to reveal a quote from Olive Schreiner. The letter in the upper-right corner of each grid square refers to the clue the letter comes from. A black square indicates the end of a word.

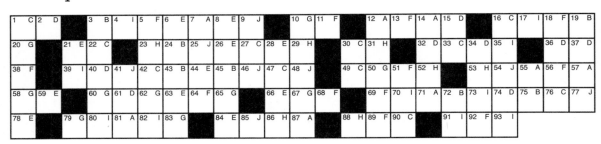

A. Impersonator

 ___ ___ ___ ___ ___ ___ ___ ___
 7   71 57 87 14 12 81 55

B. Insult

 ___ ___ ___ ___ ___ ___ ___
 43 72 3   19 24 45 75

C. Ailments or weaknesses

 ___ ___ ___ ___ ___ ___ ___ ___ ___ ___ ___
 27 47 49 76 42 1   30 16 33 90 22

D. A monarch, for one

 ___ ___ ___ ___ ___ ___ ___ ___ ___
 36 37 15 61 40 74 34 32 2

E. Florence _____

 ___ ___ ___ ___ ___ ___ ___ ___ ___ ___ ___
 28 44 78 26 84 21 8   59 66 6   63

F. Arranged or planned something big

 ___ ___ ___ ___ ___ ___ ___ ___ ___ ___ ___ ___
 51 89 69 13 18 11 56 64 92 38 5   68

G. _____ Cowboy

 ___ ___ ___ ___ ___ ___ ___ ___ ___ ___
 50 62 10 67 20 65 79 60 58 83

H. Word game involving a stick figure

 ___ ___ ___ ___ ___ ___ ___
 53 86 31 29 52 88 23

I. Like most equines

 ___ ___ ___ ___ ___ ___ ___ ___ ___ ___
 17 70 39 91 4   82 80 73 35 93

J. "_____ at the O.K. Corral"

 ___ ___ ___ ___ ___ ___ ___ ___
 9   54 77 41 46 48 85 25

Answers on page 168.

Fill in the grid with the numbers 1 through 9. Each number will be connected—horizontally or vertically—to a block of numbers all containing the same amount. So, a cell with the number 2 in it will be connected to another cell with the number 2; a cell with the number 3 will be connected to two more cells with the number 3.

	2	1			1				
			4	3			1	4	
				1	2	3		1	
2			8			4		3	
		7	7	3	1	3			
8		7			4			3	
7		3	2	1					
4	4			3	9				
			1			9	9		

NEIGHBORHOOD

Place the numbers 1 through 7 in the circles below. For each number, the sum of all the numbers connected to it is given. Numbers can only be used once.

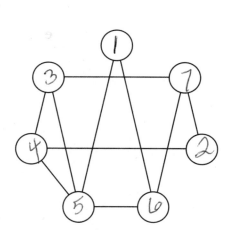

1 = 11

2 = 11

3 = 17

4 = 11

5 = 14

6 = 13

7 = 10

Answers on page 168.

MECHANIC SHOP

Tune-up your visual skills and spot the 15 differences between the top and bottom mechanic scenes.

Answers on page 168.

LOGINUMBER

Determine the values of the letters below using 2 rules: Each letter is no greater than the number of letters in the puzzle; none of the letters are equal to each other.

Use the grid to help keep track of possible solutions.

$C + E = 7$

$A > G$

$F - C = B$

$D - E = C - 2$

$B + G = D + C$

	1	2	3	4	5	6	7
A							
B							
C							
D							
E							
F							
G							

MINESWEEPER

There are 11 mines hidden in the grid. Numbers indicate the amount of mines adjacent to that square, horizontally, vertically, and diagonally. We've entered one to get you started.

Answers on page 168.

GUESS THE HOLIDAY

ACROSS

1. Difficult
5. Touch up, as text
9. Opportunity for swingers: 2 wds.
14. Southernmost Great Lake
15. Dramatic part
16. Rock pioneer Eddy
17. Old Glory: 4 wds.
20. Bill with a pyramid on the back
21. Gave the green light
22. Is in store for
23. Drug bust agents
25. Volcano in Sicily
27. Hot clue
30. Water runoff
35. "The Thin Man" dog
38. Bad _____ day
40. Take the honey and run
41. Frequent flier on the Fourth?: 3 wds.
44. "Long time _____!"
45. Pearl S. Buck's "The _____ Earth"
46. Tuna sandwich
47. Acorn creator: 2 wds.
49. IDs for the IRS
51. Concerning
53. Keep an _____ (watch closely)
57. Another name for Tarzan
61. Lyricist _____ Jay Lerner
64. "No _____" (menu phrase)
65. Patriotic Irving Berlin song: 3 wds.

68. "Fear Factor" host Joe
69. Roll call response
70. Jai follower
71. "You _____ Beautiful": Joe Cocker hit
72. Dash
73. Novice

DOWN

1. Long-legged wader
2. Fight site
3. Jockey, perhaps
4. Morning moisture
5. Estrada of "CHiPs"
6. Mollycoddle, with "on"
7. _____-France
8. Sri Lanka export
9. Kool-Aid instruction: 2 wds.
10. Marching band instrument
11. Java's neighbor
12. "Sometimes you feel like _____ ..."
13. Summer shirts, in short
18. Gardener's need
19. When repeated, Mork's phrase
24. Red wine
26. Museum sculptures
28. "So that's it!"
29. Peril
31. Like poor excuses
32. Easy gait

33. Maker of the Kadett and GT

34. Greeley's direction

35. "It will come _____ surprise..."

36. Athens portico

37. It's a piece of work

39. Words preceding a kiss: 2 wds.

42. Pfc. ID: 2 wds.

43. NFL 6-pointers: abbr.

48. Politically incorrect suffix

50. Aloha State bird

52. Artist's stand

54. Poet Dickinson

55. The Grouch of "Sesame Street"

56. Marsh of mystery

57. Taj Mahal site

58. Like Yorick

59. Sharp part of a knife

60. Many CEOs

62. Julie Christie role in "Dr. Zhivago"

63. Sermon response

66. Any boat

67. Snitch

Answers on page 168.

23

EVENS/ODDS

Arrange the numbers 2, 4, and 6 horizontally and vertically in groups of three. Similarly, arrange the numbers 1, 3, and 5 into groups of three. Combinations connect with one another on shared numbers (a vertical 135 can connect with a horizontal 513) and the even and odd numbers will intertwine.

	2		2		
5				3	
	6				4
		1			
			6		4

FIFTEEN UP

Divide the grid into 15 regions. The sum of each region must be 15. Numbers are used only once.

3	6	5	9	1	5	8
2	5	2	4	4	2	1
5	1	8	3	2	5	9
8	5	2	10	5	3	7
5	3	5	4	1	5	6
1	5	5	2	1	4	10
4	6	9	4	10	1	4

Answers on page 168.

PYTHAGORIZE IT!

Blacken one white dot within the board so that, from this dot, exactly 4 symmetrical squares can be drawn. Squares must be drawn along the black dots. See the example illustration for clarification.

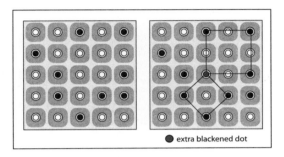

● extra blackened dot

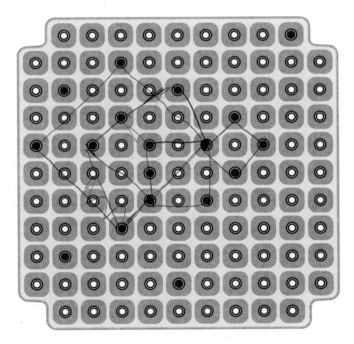

Answer on page 168.

ELEVATOR WORDS

Like an elevator, words move up and down the "floors" of this puzzle. Starting with the first answer, the second word from each answer carries down to become the first word of the following answer. With the clues given, complete the puzzle.

1. Decaf _COFFEE_
2. _COFFEE BREAK_
3. _BREAK GROUND_
4. _GROUN ROUND_
5. _ROUND ROBIN_
6. _ROBIN HOOD_
7. _HOOD_ ornament

1. Breakfast drink alternative
2. A little time off in the office
3. Start a new construction project
4. Beef buy
5. Type of tournament
6. Sherwood Forest notable
7. Auto adornment

1—7—12

CALCU-DOKU

Use arithmetic and deductive logic to complete the grid so that each row and column contains the numbers 1 through 6 in some order. Numbers in each outlined set of squares combine to produce the number in the top corner using the mathematical sign indicated.

4x	2x		3-	30x	
	4	10x		1-	
2/			1-	15x	2/
5-		12x			
10x	5		3+	5+	10+
	9+				

Answers on page 169.

SPLIT DECISIONS

Fill in each set of empty cells with letters that will create English words reading both across and down. Letters may repeat within a single set. We've completed one set to get you started.

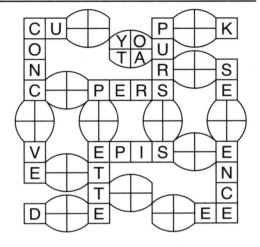

NUMBER CROSSWORD

Fill in this crossword with numbers instead of letters. Use the clues to determine which number from 1 through 9 belongs in each square. No zeros are used.

ACROSS

1. Its middle digit is the sum of its first and last digits
4. Consecutive digits, descending
5. The cube of its first digit is the 3-digit number formed by its last 3-digits
6. Three identical digits

DOWN

1. The sum of its first 2 digits is equal to the sum of its last 2 digits
2. Consecutive digits, in some order
3. A multiple of 17
4. A perfect cube
5. A multiple of 23

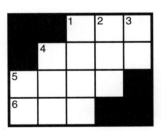

Answers on page 169.

CONTINUOUS

Below is a chain of continuous words. Start at clue number 1 and write the answers to the clues in the order they are given. Every answer overlaps the next one by one letter or more. If done correctly, the shaded rows will spell out 5 types of fabrics.

1. Cicatrix
2. A firearm
3. Always
4. Cooking directions
5. Hire
6. Adolescence
7. Warmth
8. Recorded
9. U.S. currency
10. Regal
11. Change
12. Tall water plant
13. A sea mammal
14. Sister
15. Birds' homes
16. Ought to
17. Uses a car
18. Pollution fog
19. Legendary monsters
20. Body of water
21. Room under a roof
22. Join together

23. Cease-fire
24. Tooth covering
25. Small
26. European volcano

27. Woe is me
28. Spread, smudged
29. Decline, drop

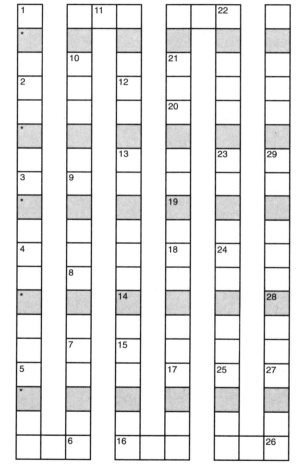

Answers on page 169.

QUIPU

Which of the 3 Quipus (Incan devices for recording information) is identical to the one in the frame? Quipus are considered identical when they can be matched perfectly only by rotating pieces around the knots—they cannot be lifted or turned over. See the examples for further clarification.

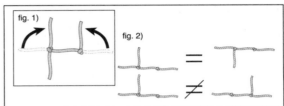

fig. 1)

fig. 2)

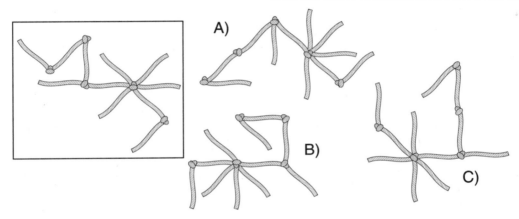

A)

B)

C)

CROSS SUMS

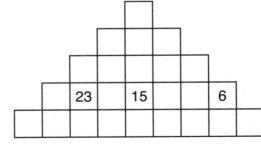

Use the numbers below to fill in the grid. Each cell at the top of the 3 adjacent cells is the sum of numbers below it. So, as seen in the example, A=B+C+D. Here's the numbers needed to fill in the bottom 2 rows:

	A	
B	C	D

1 2 3 4 5 6 7 8 9 9 12 18 24

Answers on page 169.

WORD JIGSAW

Fit the pieces into the frame to form common words reading across and down. There's no need to rotate the pieces; they'll fit as shown, with each piece used once.

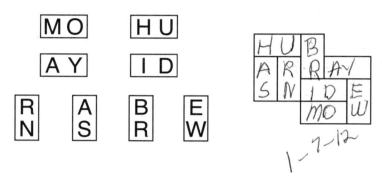

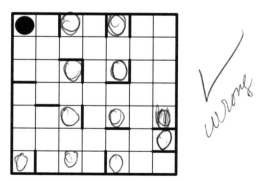

MARBLES

Place 13 marbles into the grid without having any touch one another, not even diagonally. There are some walls, represented by thick lines, that block the view of the marbles. Marbles must not "see" each other in a horizontal or vertical direction. We've placed one to get you started.

Answers on page 169.

SUDOKU

Use deductive logic to complete the grid so that each row, each column, and each 3 by 3 box contains the numbers 1 through 9 in some order. The solution is unique.

							8	
	5			6	3	9	1	
	8		2					5
	1			5				3
3			9		8			1
5				7			4	
8					7		9	
	6	1	5	9			3	
	9							

VEX-A-GON

Place the numbers 1 through 6 into the triangles of each hexagon. The numbers may be in any order, but they do not repeat within each hexagon shape.

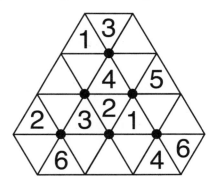

Answers on page 169.

CURVE FILL

Fill in each heavy-outlined set of cells with the same number (0, 2, or 5) so that the sums given for each curved row and column and the 2 sections extending from the center oval are true. For further insight, see the example puzzle at right.

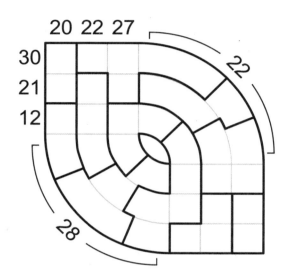

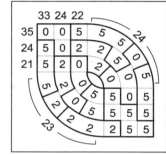

ADDAGRAM

This puzzle functions exactly like an anagram (a word that is a rearrangement of another word) with an added step: In addition to being scrambled, each word below is missing the same letter. Discover the missing letter and then unscramble the words. When you do, you'll reveal pincers, a metal, a fast-running animal, and a native of a country.

SWEETER

BORNE

ALLEGE

INCITE

Answers on page 170.

HONEYCOMB

Answer each definition with a 6-letter word. Write the words in either a clockwise or counterclockwise direction around the numerals in the grid. We've placed some letters to get you started.

CLOCKWISE

2. In poor health
3. Discontinues
5. Old-time garments
7. Weasel's cousin
11. Beer container
12. Matched set of clothes
14. Musical productions
15. Irregularly shaped spot
17. Barbed remarks
18. Hates
19. Bug
20. Process, as food
21. Numerical relationships
25. Strand
26. Flavoring seed
27. Slurs over
28. Quantity
30. One sex
34. Tactless acts
35. Bucolic
36. Spill forth
37. Pixie

COUNTERCLOCKWISE

1. Cut portion of food
4. Wine and dine
6. Appeared to be

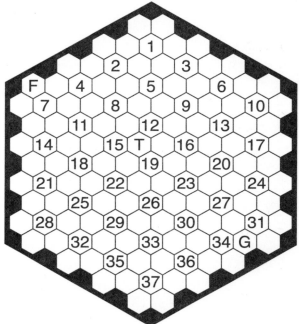

8. Waiting room
9. Most uninhibited
10. Like a two-seater bike
13. Slightest
16. Part of a hand
22. Select
23. Straightens
24. Socially virtuous
29. Burdens
31. Refined manners
32. One way to set sail
33. Hold in high regard

Answers on page 170.

FITTING WORDS

In this miniature crossword, the clues are listed randomly and are numbered for convenience only. It is up to you to figure out the placement of the 9 answers. To help you, we've inserted one letter in the grid, and this is the only occurrence of that letter in the completed puzzle.

CLUES

1. Wheel shaft
2. Banishment
3. Box-office bomb
4. Shipbuilding wood
5. Candy that gets pulled
6. Certain evergreens
7. Manicurist's tool

8. Permit
9. Hangs on to

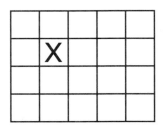

HITORI

The object of this puzzle is to have a number appear only once in each row and column. By shading a number cell, you are effectively removing that number from its row and column. There's a catch though: Shaded number cells are never adjacent to one another in a row or column.

2	5	9	5	6	1	3	1	8
8	7	2	2	9	9	6	4	1
7	8	5	3	2	1	9	3	4
1	4	3	1	2	6	5	5	2
9	4	2	4	8	1	5	3	6
6	9	3	4	1	7	5	2	6
5	6	7	4	4	5	1	8	3
3	1	1	6	9	8	7	8	9
4	3	3	7	9	2	9	6	8

Answers on page 170.

WORD-A-MAZE: A ZOO IN A BOX

Travel in sequence through the puzzle from the left side to the right, using each numbered clue to determine the correct word. Connect adjacent words together with a common letter to proceed through the maze. Some letters are already given. The first and last words tie into the title.

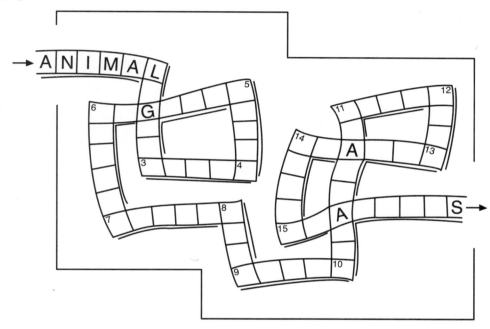

1. Mammal

2. Army group

3. Silky substitute

4. Dark of day

5. Brain work

6. Claws

7. Brother and _____

8. Woody stalk

9. Not angel

10. Dedicated followers

11. Audible

12. Not smart

13. Relax

14. Sleight of hand

15. Salted wafers

Answers on page 170.

MEND THE BRIDGES

Rain has swept through the entire county, flooding all the bridges (indicated by circles). Your job is to travel to each location—**A** through **I,** in any order—by restoring only 2 of the bridges.

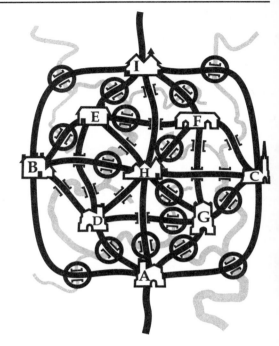

FUTOSHIKI

Place the numbers 1 through 6 in each row and column. Numbers do not repeat in any row or column. Inequality restraints (less-than and greater-than symbols) must be met when placing numbers.

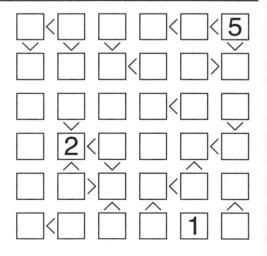

Answers on page 170.

KAKURO

Place a number from 1 through 9 in each empty cell so that the sum of each vertical or horizontal run (rows and columns extending from already numbered cells) equals the number at the top or on the left of that run. Numbers may not be repeated in any run, and runs end at dark-colored squares.

SQUARO

Shade in circles around each square as indicated by the numbers. For example, a square with a number 3 in it will have 3 of the 4 connected circles shaded in.

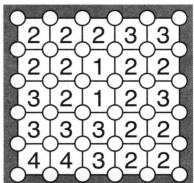

Answers on pages 170–171.

CHAIN SUDOKU

Use deductive logic to complete the grid so that each row, each column, and each connected set of circles contains the numbers 1 through 6 in some order. The solution is unique.

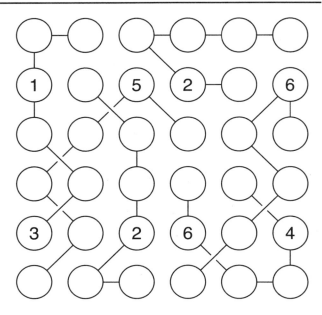

PERFECT SCORE

Make 3 successful hits so that the sum of the numbers is 100. Double and triple scores do not apply. Numbers may be used more than once.

Answers on page 171.

GRAMMY HALL OF FAME AWARDS

The grid contains the names of artists whose recordings have received Grammy Hall of Fame Awards. Words can be found in a straight line horizontally, vertically, or diagonally. They may be read either backward or forward. The leftover letters spell out an additional fact.

AL JOLSON

ANDRES SEGOVIA

ARTIE SHAW

THE BEACH BOYS

BING CROSBY

BOBBY DARIN

BOB DYLAN

CHUCK BERRY

COUNT BASIE

DEAN MARTIN

THE DOORS

EDITH PIAF

ELLA FITZGERALD

ELVIS PRESLEY

FATS DOMINO

FATS WALLER

GENE AUTRY

GLENN GOULD

JOHN COLTRANE

JUDY GARLAND

LENA HORNE

MILES DAVIS

PATSY CLINE

PRINCE

RAY CHARLES

SANTANA

```
G L E N N G O U L D T H I S I S A
P A I V O G E S S E R D N A A R T
I S S A L L I S T D O S P F L T H
E E A J O H N C O L T R A N E D O
Z L B B O B D Y L A N O T E N N N
Y R T U A E N E G R F O S J A I S
M A N O A Y F L Y E A D Y U H R N
I H U P R R P S B G T E C D O A I
L C O S T R E E S Z S H L Y R D T
E Y C A I E D R O T W T I G N Y R
S A E N E B I P R I A R N A E B A
D R C T S K T S C F L F E R O B M
A E R A H C H I G A L J O L S O N
V M E N A U P V N L E R S A H B A
I O N A W H I L I L R O R N E D E
S Y O B H C A E B E H T B D Y T D
H E A W A R F A T S D O M I N O D
```

Hidden fact: _____

Answers on page 171.

STRETCH!

ACROSS

1. Like some wines or cheeses
5. Make a selection
8. "But _____ counting?"
12. Downtown ride, perhaps
13. Sign compatible with Sagittarius
14. Not just yours or mine
15. "Jumpin' Jack Flash, it's _____ ..."
16. Michigan city nicknamed "A Squared": 2 wds.
18. It's stretched if you gently tilt your head forward: 3 wds.
20. General on a Chinese menu
21. Hagar the Horrible's wife
25. Key that helps you exit: abbr.
27. It's stretched if you sit with one leg straight out, bend the opposite leg, cross the opposite foot over, and pull the opposite knee across your body toward your shoulder
31. Sight on a clear night
33. Drink that's steeped
34. Dirty reading material
35. They're stretched if you put your right hand on your left shoulder, then pull the right elbow across your chest toward your left shoulder and hold (then vice versa)
38. Double curve
39. "OK, if you _____ ..."
40. Crow call
42. It's stretched if you grasp the top of your left foot with your right hand, pull your heel up
48. Brilliant examples
51. Garfield's dog pal
52. Prefix before "dextrous"
53. Actor Patel of "Slumdog Millionaire"
54. "_____ Weak" (Belinda Carlisle song)
55. Vixen's musical genre
56. King's equivalent: abbr.
57. The Loch _____ Monster

DOWN

1. Run _____ (accumulate charges from the bar)
2. "Poker Face" singer Lady _____
3. It's no different from the original in any way: 2 wds.
4. Computer storage items
5. Lemony Snicket's villainous count
6. "Milk" star Sean
7. Vocal quality
8. Staff
9. Airline's central city
10. Gold, in Guatemala
11. Armenia or Kazakhstan, pre-1991: abbr.

17. Eight, in Germany
19. "You're in trou-ble!" noise
22. Citrusy addition to a mixed drink: 2 wds.
23. Wildebeests' kin
24. CIA staffers: abbr.
25. They stay grounded Down Under
26. Soup, on a Mexican menu
28. _____ loss for words
29. Debussy's "La _____"
30. Alice's boyfriend, on "The Brady Bunch"
32. Chocolate-flavored milk mix with a bunny mascot

36. Disastrous defeat
37. _____-fi (fiction genre)
41. At the flip of: 2 wds.
43. Congressional assistant
44. Consider (worthy)
45. Invitation request: abbr.
46. Slapstick projectiles
47. Play backdrops
48. Place where pick-up lines are practiced
49. Genre of music where guys may wear "guyliner"
50. "Desperate Housewives" network

Answers on page 171.

Use each of the words, names, and acronyms listed here to complete this clue-less crossword grid. The puzzle has only one solution.

3 Letters
ETC
PIN
RUN
TAR

4 Letters
ALOE
BARN
BYTE
CALM
DOOR
EDEN
GURU
HOPE
JIVE
LILY
OPAL
SCAN
SLUG
TUNA
UNDO
USED

NOTES
PEACE
PIANO
READY
SPACE
TANGO
TWEAK
UMBER
WHIRL

6 Letters
CAJOLE
CIRCLE
CLEAVE
EARWIG
EGOIST
FEDORA
HERBAL
PACKET
PARROT
REBATE
SKETCH
TAILOR

5 Letters
BAGEL
BAKER
CRUMB
EMPTY
LATIN
LILAC
MOOSE

7 Letters
AWESOME
CAJOLE
CURRANT
LOBSTER
MORELLO
NETBALL
OREGANO

PALERMO
PASTURE
RESERVE
RISSOLE
UTENSIL

8 Letters
JAMBOREE
SANDWICH

9 Letters
CHALLENGE
FRAGRANCE
IRREGULAR
LANDSCAPE
PRESIDENT
STALEMATE

Answer on page 171.

WORD COLUMNS

Find the hidden humorous observation by using the letters directly below each of the blank squares. Each letter is used only once. A black square indicates the end of a word.

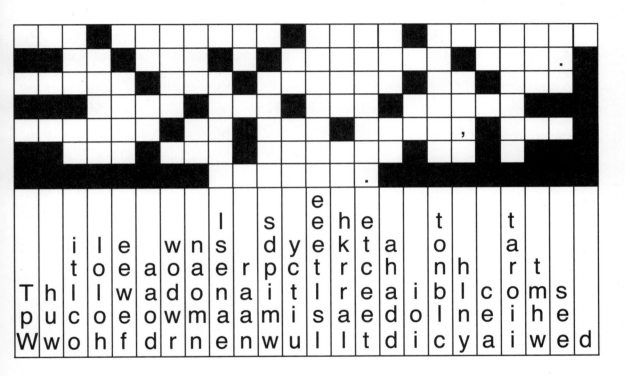

TRIVIA ON THE BRAIN
Prolonged stress can kill cells in the hippo-campus, the part of your brain that's critical for memory. Thankfully, we're able to grow new neurons in this area again, even as adults.

Answer on page 171.

Shown are 9 mutation chambers surrounded by alien figures. Each of the 3 aliens on the left passed through the 3 chambers to their right and transformed into the figure on the other side (e.g. the alien on the left of A passed through chambers A, B, and C and mutated into the alien to the right of C). The same is true for the aliens above the chambers: Each passed through the 3 chambers directly below them and came out mutated on the other side.

Each chamber affects one—and only one—alteration (changes in head or body shape, changes in posture, addition/removal of appendages). Note: Some chambers in the same row or column may undo what a previous chamber has done.

What mutation is each chamber responsible for?

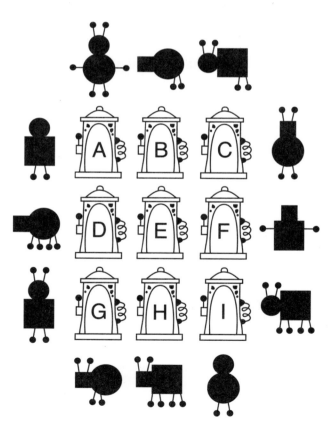

Answers on page 171.

KLUMP

Shade in some of the numbers so the remaining connected sets of numbers match the following sums:

1, 6, 7, 8, 9, 10, 15, 20

A solitary number (not connected to any other) can represent one or more of these sums.

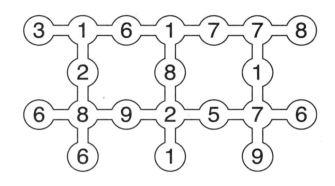

HASHI

Each circle represents an island, with the number inside indicating the number of bridges connected to it. Draw bridges between islands using the number given. There can be no more than 2 bridges going in the same direction, and there must be a continuous path connecting all islands. Bridges can only be vertical or horizontal and may not cross islands or other bridges. We've drawn some bridges to get you started.

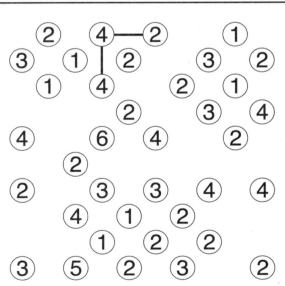

Answers on page 172.

ABCD

Every cell in this grid contains 1 of 4 letters: A, B, C, or D. No letter can be horizontally or vertically adjacent to itself. The tables above and to the left of the grid indicate how many times each letter appears in that column or row. Can you complete the grid?

				A	1	0	3	1	0	2
				B	1	2	0	2	1	2
				C	2	2	1	2	3	2
A	B	C	D		2	2	2	1	2	0
0	3	2	1							
2	0	2	2							
2	1	2	1					B		
1	1	2	2							
0	1	2	3							
2	2	2	0							

Answer on page 172.

CUBE FOLD

Which 3 of the 4 patterns can be folded into the cube seen at center?

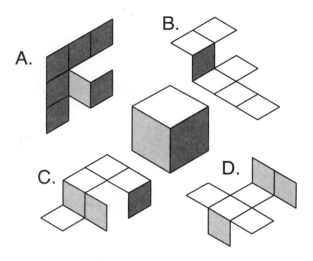

WORD JIGSAW

Fit the pieces into the frame to form common words reading across and down. There's no need to rotate the pieces; they'll fit as shown, with each piece used once.

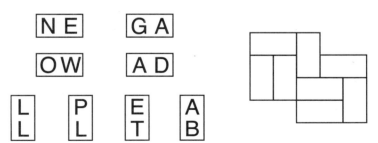

Answers on page 172.

KNOT PROBLEM

Which 2 of the 3 rings of string contain knots, A, B, or C? Study the example below for help on knotted and unknotted string. The figure on the left is unknotted; the figure on the right is knotted.

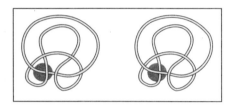

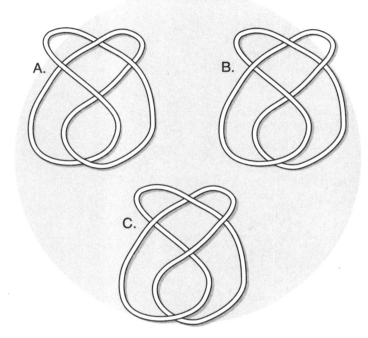

VEX-A-GON

Place the numbers 1 through 6 into the triangles of each hexagon. The numbers may be in any order, but they do not repeat within each hexagon shape.

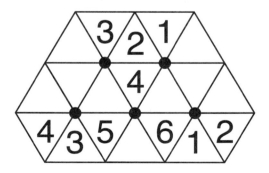

Answers on page 172.

RED, WHITE, AND BLUE

Each row, column, and long diagonal contains 2 reds, 2 whites, and 2 blues. From the clues given below, can you complete the grid?

1. No clue needed.

2. No clue needed.

3. Two reds and a blue are directly enclosed by whites.

4. The pattern of colors takes the form abcacb.

5. No clue needed.

6. There are no blues or reds in the outer cells.

A. Each blue is directly above each red.

B. No clue needed.

C. Each white is directly above each red.

D. No clue needed.

E. The reds are adjacent.

F. A blue and a red are directly enclosed by the whites.

```
    A B C D E F
1
2
3
4
5
6
```

TRIVIA ON THE BRAIN
People who have damage in their brain's frontal lobe may not be able to judge when the punch line of a joke is funny.

Answer on page 172.

CROSS SCAN

Think of this puzzle as a crossword/word search hybrid. Answer each of the clues (numbers in parentheses indicate the numbers of letters in the answer), and then find the word in the letter grid on the next page. If you get stumped, scan the letter grid for words, and try to see if they match the clues.

This puzzle also has a hidden theme, which will be revealed as you get closer to completion. Leftover letters spell out a saying that ties in with the theme.

1. Fresh (3)

2. Peppermint patty maker (4)

3. Metropolis (4)

4. Anagram for "stem" (4)

5. Green area (4)

6. Big piano (5)

7. _____ hand (advantage) (5)

8. Nile or Danube (5)

9. FM or ham (5)

10. Song or sonata (5)

11. "Aida", e.g. (5)

12. Smithsonian is one (6)

13. Globetrotters home (6)

14. Batman's city (6)

15. Holy Roman _____ (6)

16. Love site (6)

17. Huge men (6)

18. Sandwich shop (6)

19. Chessboard component (6)

20. "No man is an _____" (6)

21. Card game (6)

22. Fourth president (7)

23. Young Mrs. Clinton (7)

24. "It takes a _____" (7)

25. AA or 9-volt (7)

26. U.S. time zone (7)

27. Mantle team (7)

28. Hebrew school (7)

29. Park officials (7)

30. Part of "CBS" (8)

31. Tycoon Andrew _____ (8)

32. Huge macintosh (8)

33. Dutch city (9)

34. Woody Allen film (9)

35. Prime meridian site (9)

36. Nicholson movie (9)

37. State or D.C. (10)

```
G B R I D G E G A L L I V W P
T O H E H C I W N E E R G A E
S C T S M I H E R L N T R S I
T O I H Q S C I T Y N K B H G
E L R N A U P G N P U A O I E
M U E S U M A N H A T T A N N
T M V C E A A R S T T N O G R
A B I L O D G D E R T O K T A
V I R Y O R K R I S E S W O C
I A U A I E Y P A S A G D N E
H R R N D T I C U N O H N C N
S E R K A S E B A T D N A A T
E P W E R M W R E P P U L I R
Y O E E V A E S C H E L S E A
T E N S Y W E L P P A G I B L
```

Leftover letters: _____

Theme: _____

Answers on page 172.

SLITHERLINK PATH

Create a single continuous path along the dotted lines. The path does not cross itself or touch at any corners. Numbers indicate how many line segments surround each cell. We've filled in some line segments to get you started.

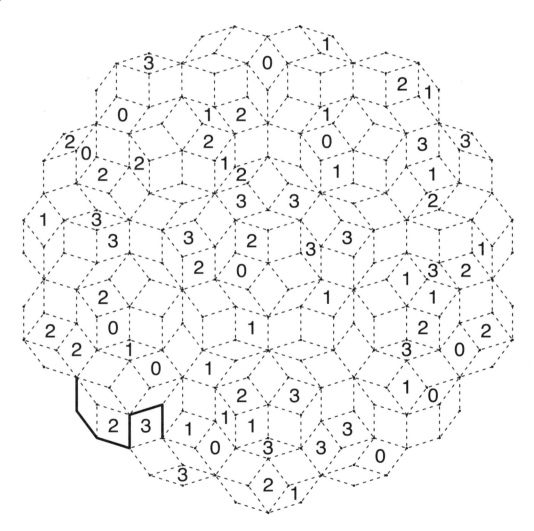

Answer on page 173.

FILLOMINO

Fill in the grid with the numbers 1 through 8. Each number will be connected—horizontally or vertically—to a block of numbers all containing the same amount. So a cell with the number 2 in it will be connected to another cell with the number 2; a cell with the number 3 will be connected to two more cells with the number 3.

		7		7			3	7
				7				
	4					8	6	6
					6	6		4
	7		2	1	8		6	
4		3	3					
1	7	7					3	
				4				
8	8			4		4		

FIFTEEN UP

Divide the grid into 15 regions. The sum of each region must be 15. Numbers are used only once.

4	5	7	5	5	3	9
2	2	3	5	1	2	7
2	5	4	9	8	2	6
1	3	8	6	6	1	3
1	6	6	12	3	1	10
5	7	9	1	1	12	2
1	2	3	4	11	1	3

Answers on page 173.

STAR POWER

Fill in each of the empty squares in the grid so that each star is surrounded by the numbers 1 through 8 with no repeats.

	5	1	8					
8	★	7	★	5	8	2		7
3	2		3		★	1	★	4
7	★		★			6		
6		8			★		★	4
	1	★	4	★		2		1	3
	6		7	3	6	★	8	★	7
					7	4	6	

TRIVIA ON THE BRAIN

Researches think that the mental capacity of a 100-year-old person who has perfect memory could be represented by a computer with 10 to the power of 15 bits (one petabit). At the rate technology is growing today, that figure will probably be attainable in about 35 years. One caveat: This just represents memory capacity, not thought creation or emotions, which are extremely complex.

Answer on page 173.

MASTERMIND

The goal of this puzzle is to replace the question marks with a correct sequence of numbers. The numbers you need for the answer are contained in the rows above the question marks. Follow these 2 guides: A black dot indicates that a number needed for the solution is in that row and in the correct position; a white dot means that a number needed for the solution is in that row but in the wrong position. Numbers do not appear more than once in the solution, and the solution never begins with 0.

```
2 5 4 6 3   ● ● ● ○
3 8 7 1 2   ○ ○ ○
1 4 5 9 0   ○ ○
9 8 7 6 5   ●
─────────
? ? ? ? ?
```

TIMES SQUARE

Fill in each empty cell of the grid with a number between 1 and 9. The product (multiplication) of the numbers in each row must be the value to the right of that row of the grid, and the product of each column must be the value below that column of the grid.

Important: The number 1 can only be used once in any row or column; other numbers can be repeated.

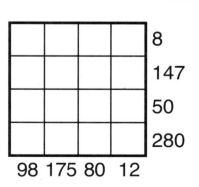

Answers on page 173.

1-2-3

Place the numbers 1, 2, or 3 in the empty circles. The challenge is to have only these 3 numbers in each connected row and column—no number should repeat. Any combination is allowed.

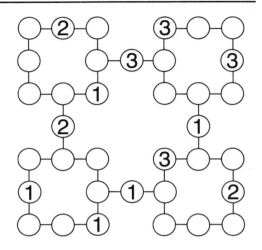

CRYPTO-LOGIC

Each of the numbers in the sequence below represents a letter. Use the mathematical clues to determine which number stands for which letter and reveal the encrypted word.

5723

Clues:

L = 10   S = 1

L ÷ N = D   D + 2 = O

D − 4 = S   D − N = E

Answers on page 173.

ADD-A-LETTER

This is a standard word search with a twist: For each word in the list, you must add one letter to form a new word, which you will then search for in the grid. For example: If the listed word is CARTON, you'd search for CARTOON; if the listed word is OTTER, you might have to search for HOTTER or POTTER.

The words can be found in a straight line horizontally, vertically, or diagonally, and may read backward or forward.

ACTOR
ADDLE
BEAD
BORER
BOTHER
CAMP
CAPE
CASH
CASTER
CAVE
COOK
CURE
DANGER
DEIGN
DROP
ELATE

ERROR
FACTION
FAIR
GRATER
HERO
JUST
LUNGE
PARK
PARTY
PATENT
PATH
POPLAR
POSSES
PUSH
REASON
REVEL

```
W B R O T H E R B O R D E R E
P O S S E S S F A K I R V O K
L G Z G S P A R K J S A R U O
U D N N M R J D O P E E U S O
N R J I P O P U L A R B C E R
G E E K R U S I N G L I N G C
E T N L R T C E R E L A T E M
X A O A G E S E V A R C N A N
U E I W K N A L H L T K E G O
H W T Y C T A D P C O R I X R
S S C R E N O D N E T S T D E
U P A R T L Y A O S E A A R H
L M R L S C A P E D M W P O G
P O F A C T O R T R E A S O N
R E V E A L C O A S T E R P J
```

RUSE
SEAT
SEEP
SINGING
SLICE

SOLE
SPOUT
STEAM

STING
TENON
WAKING

Answers on page 173.

ON YOUR MARK, GET SET...

Go! And be sure to find the 10 differences between these scenes along the way.

Answers on page 173.

ACROSS THE BOARD

Fill in the grid with a path of consecutive numbers starting at 1 and ending at 49. Numbers may connect vertically, horizontally, or diagonally.

	44		29	28	25	
	42			32		24
						21
39	40			47		20
				7		
		(49)				
13	14			(1)		

GRID FILL

To complete this puzzle, place the given letters and words into the shapes in this grid. Words and letters will run across, down, and wrap around each shape. When the grid is filled, each row will contain one of the following words: ample, arson, igloo, Spain, strip, vests.

1. I, S, T

2. GL, IS, LE

3. NON

4. RAMP, SAVE

5. PAIRS, STOOP

Answers on page 174.

GLOBE QUEST

Fly from Miami to Seattle, visiting each city once. See if you can find the cheapest route for your trip. Less than $450 would make you a Super Vacationer; less than $430, a Passport Pioneer; less than $400, a Seasoned Traveler. If you can make the trip for $370, then you're a Globe Quester!

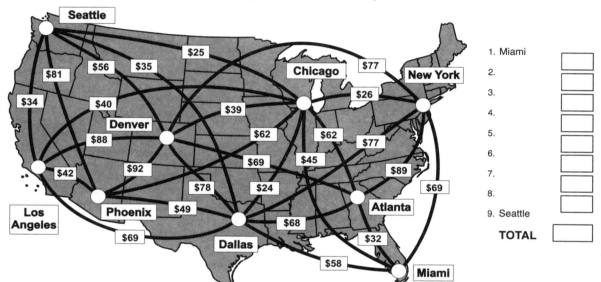

1. Miami
2.
3.
4.
5.
6.
7.
8.
9. Seattle

TOTAL

MEND THE BRIDGES

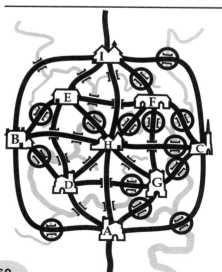

Rain has swept through the entire county, flooding all the bridges (indicated by circles). Your job is to travel to each location—**A** through **I**, in any order—by restoring only 2 of the bridges.

Answers on page 174.

BATTLE BOATS

Place each ship in the fleet located at right within the grid. Ships may be placed horizontally or vertically, but they don't touch each other, not even diagonally. Numbers reveal the ship segments located in that row or column. Some segments have been added to get you started.

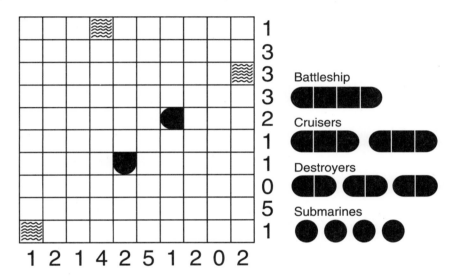

1
3
3
3
2
1
1
0
5
1

1 2 1 4 2 5 1 2 0 2

Battleship

Cruisers

Destroyers

Submarines

VEX-A-GON

Place the numbers 1 through 6 into the triangles of each hexagon. The numbers may be in any order but they do not repeat within each hexagon shape.

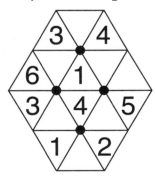

Answers on page 174.

MINESWEEPER

There are 30 mines hidden in the grid. Numbers indicate the amount of mines adjacent to that square, horizontally, vertically, and diagonally. We've entered one to get you started.

2			1			1			2
	2	1					2		
	1		2			2	1		
2			3			2			2
							1	1	
		1			1				
2		2	2			3			2
		✹		1					3
	4				1				
2			1			1	2		2

ADDAGRAM

This puzzle functions exactly like an anagram (a word that is a rearrangement of another word) with an added step: In addition to being scrambled, each word below is missing the same letter. Discover the missing letter and then unscramble the words. When you do, you'll reveal a ceremony, something central, profitable, and charitable.

TRAIL

UNCLES

VERTICAL

MISTRAL

Answers on page 174.

NEIGHBORHOOD

Place the numbers 1 through 6 in the circles below. For each number, the sum of all the numbers connected to it is given. Numbers can only be used once.

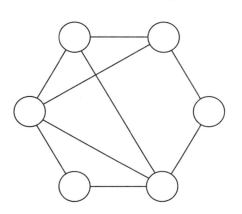

$\left(1\right)$ = 11

$\left(2\right)$ = 15

$\left(3\right)$ = 10

$\left(4\right)$ = 10

$\left(5\right)$ = 13

$\left(6\right)$ = 11

LOGIDOKU

The numbers 1 through 9 appear once in every row, column, long diagonal, irregular shape (indicated by marked borders), and 3 by 3 grid. From the numbers already given, can you complete the puzzle?

6			1					
						3		
		9						
					2			7
1		6				9		
				4				
	5						3	
			7		8			

Answers on pages 174–175.

XOXO

Place an X or an O inside each empty cell of the grid so that there appears no row, column, or diagonal with 4 consecutive cells with the same letter.

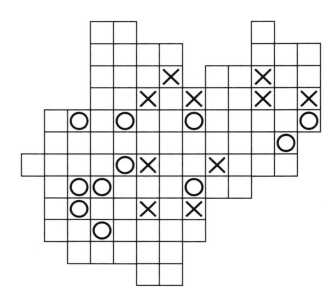

HASHI

Each circle represents an island, with the number inside indicating the number of bridges connected to it. Draw bridges between islands using the number given. There can be no more than 2 bridges going in the same direction, and there must be a continuous path connecting all islands. Bridges can only be vertical or horizontal and may not cross islands or other bridges. We've drawn some bridges to get you started.

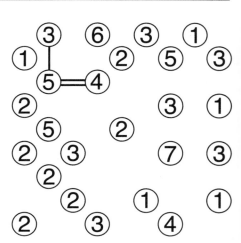

Answers on page 175.

STARSTRUCK

Journey from Earth (E) to Mars (Ma), hitting all the other planets along the way. Keep track of the days it takes to travel between planets using the empty boxes below.

If you are able to make the trip in 28 or more days, you are a Promising Pilot; 27 days, a Nifty Navigator; less than 24 days, an Amazing Astronaut; do it in 21 days, and you'll be a Master of the Universe!

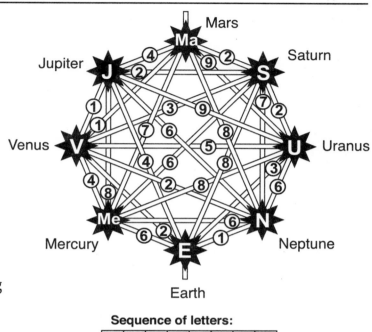

Sequence of letters:

E						Ma

Days by spacecraft:

						=	

SQUARO

Shade in circles around each square as indicated by the numbers. For example, a square with a number 3 in it will have 3 of the 4 connected circles shaded in.

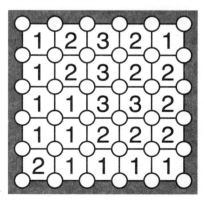

Answers on page 175.

FITTING WORDS

In this miniature crossword, the clues are listed randomly and are numbered for convenience only. It is up to you to figure out the placement of the 9 answers. To help you, we've inserted one letter in the grid, and this is the only occurrence of that letter in the completed puzzle.

CLUES

1. Liquor to-go holder

2. Like the "c" in "certain"

3. Canvas shelters

4. Acts as quizmaster

5. Orchestral instruments

6. Fit for duty

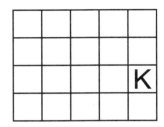

7. Brazilian dance

8. Cream of the crop

9. Haunted house sound

FRAME GAMES™

Can you "read" the phrase below?

WORD^{yy} = enough

Answers on page 175.

FLOWERS

The letters in AZALEA can be found in boxes 8, 13, 14, and 22 but not necessarily in that order. Similarly, the letters in all the other types of flowers can be found in the boxes indicated. Your task is to insert all the letters of the alphabet into the boxes. If you do this correctly, the shaded cells will reveal the name of another type of flower.

Hint: Compare PEONY and TULIP to get the value of **P**, then TULIP and MYRTLE for the value of **T**.

1	2	3	4	5	6	7	8	9	10	11	12	13

14	15	16	17	18	19	20	21	22	23	24	25	26

AZALEA: 8, 13, 14, 22

BUTTERCUP: 2, 3, 11, 13, 15, 19, 21

CHRYSANTHEMUM: 2, 3, 4, 11, 12, 13, 14, 17, 19, 20, 24

DAFFODIL: 1, 5, 6, 14, 22, 25

FOXGLOVE: 1, 9, 13, 22, 23, 25, 26

GLOXINIA: 1, 5, 9, 14, 17, 22, 23

HONEYSUCKLE: 1, 3, 4, 12, 13, 16, 17, 19, 20, 22

JASMINE: 5, 7, 12, 13, 14, 17, 24

JONQUIL: 1, 5, 7, 17, 18, 19, 22

MYRTLE: 2, 11, 13, 20, 22, 24

PEONY: 1, 13, 17, 20, 21

SMILAX: 5, 9, 12, 14, 22, 24

TULIP: 5, 11, 19, 21, 22

WISTERIA: 2, 5, 10, 11, 12, 13, 14

ZINNIA: 5, 8, 14, 17

Answers on page 175.

WATER TANKS

Each cubic tank holds 6 gallons of water. Fill in some of the tanks with water to satisfy the volume given in the rows and columns. Equilibrium must be met within each outlined set of tanks. Note that some tanks in rows or columns without specified amounts may be filled to meet this need.

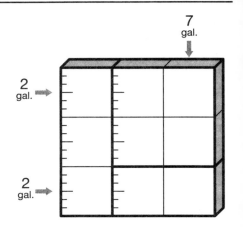

MINESWEEPER

There are 20 mines hidden in the grid. Numbers indicate the amount of mines adjacent to that square, horizontally, vertically, and diagonally. We've entered one to get you started.

Answers on page 175.

The letters of the alphabet are hidden in code: They are represented by a random number from 1 through 26. With the letters already given, complete the crossword puzzle with English words and break the code.

	18		26		24		4		10		19	
18	13	24	20	12	15		7	14	7	17	16	23
	20		15		10		5		20		21	
16	19	15	18		7	24	24	16	8	7	23	25
		25		22		18		9		25		
3	20	13	5	25	15	24		25	5	6	5	7
	13		16		19		19		23		14	
18	9	16	23	15		21	15	5	8	9	15	19
	15		23		25		12		18			
12	7	11	7	10	5	15	24		25	15	18	25
	11		5		10		1		16		2	
3	7	24	24	15	19		13	5	12	23	5	12
	10		15		15		25		2		19	

A B C D E F G H I J K L M N O P Q R S T U V W X Y Z

1	2	3	4	5	6	7	8	9	10	11	12	13
Y							G		L			

14	15	16	17	18	19	20	21	22	23	24	25	26
		O				U						

Answer on page 176.

SHROUDED SUMMARY

Hidden in the word search is a summary of a well-known novel. The words you need to find are listed below; in the word search they are presented in an order that makes more sense. The words may be vertical, horizontal, or diagonal. As a bonus, can you name the novel and its author?

ALIENS

AND

APPEAR

BOMBING

DRESDEN

DURING

ENCOUNTERS

EXPERIENCE

FUTURE

HIS

INHERITING

JUMPING

PAST

PRESENT

PRISONER

RANDOMLY

SECOND

TIME

WAR

WHERE

WORLD

```
G N I R U D A O E V K W N K L F I E
V C R O R U R C R P E Z L S W S L I
I N E E E R O E Y T D R N I I R D G
H A S E K I E S S O M R P A N S V N
J S O U I M L E W D L T I E D N T E
R O H L A F I C I A E N S O I R O R
L A N R M O B O M B I N G N I W H R
S E O O X Z L N T P A R I T U H C N
I D I W O R L D A W H L B E D S E H
R I A J E R A N O I N A L I U T E N
P R I S O N E R T A E S B J S T R W
T N T O E U C P I L O T Y T I D P S
S W G C H T P O M I L B O H M I B O
N T Y C H A D V U E B V O C C O M C
T N I G N P E R E N A Q P A E W R A
P L T I E J J N T S T C O U H C R A
O T D D E T N U I N H E R I T I N G
R A N Y L F T E M R S E R C T P Y A
M B G A D E R W E P A P P S I O L I
V E R T P A R H E H I N G E O I M A
R O P F E X P E R I E N C E E F O T
P L M A L A I R E S N L G D E F D E
A E D O S N S E E R A F N R I P N R
B E L T S T P O A S T I E I N L A N
G I U T U F U T U R E A P P E A R N
E N I E N S O S K S T N A R A M D B
O I F R C N A B H I T D T O D I E O
```

Novel and author: _____

Answers on page 176.

KAKURO

Place a number from 1 through 9 in each empty cell so that the sum of each vertical or horizontal run (rows and columns extending from already numbered cells) equals the number at the top or on the left of that run. Numbers may not be repeated in any run, and runs end at dark-colored squares.

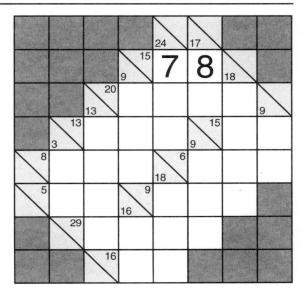

WORD LADDER

Use the clues to change just one letter on each line to go from the top word to the bottom word. Do not change the order of the letters. You must have a common English word at each step.

BRUSH

_____ rude and uncouth

_____ collision

_____ disharmonious colors

_____ gentility

_____ rude and dirty-minded

BRASS

Answers on page 176.

CONTINUOUS

Starting at the top left corner, place all the numbers in a continuous chain. The last digit of one number is the first digit of the following number.

01882

09164

10218

13867

21959

28297

40035

43618

55281

65251

65410

73420

77618

81345

83702

84516

90634

96836

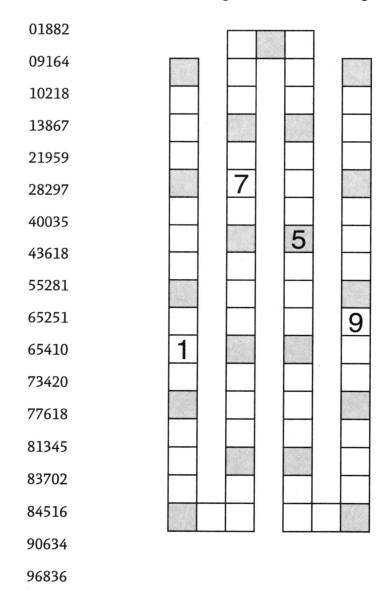

Answer on page 176.

PERFECT SCORE

Make 3 successful hits so that the sum of the numbers is 100. Double and triple scores do not apply. Numbers may be used more than once.

WORD JIGSAW

Fit the pieces into the frame to form common words reading across and down. There's no need to rotate the pieces; they'll fit as shown, with each piece used once.

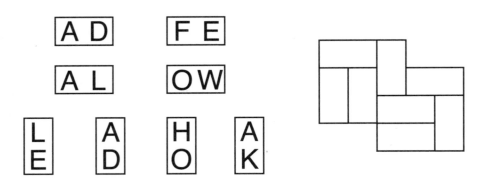

Answers on page 176.

OPEN UP!

ACROSS

1. Wine glass part
5. 1982 Disney computer movie
9. Clingy lizard
14. 2003 film "_____ Actually"
15. Where the first presidential caucus takes place
16. Out of style
17. Idyllic place
18. Primate revered by French worshipers?: 2 wds.
20. Strauss's river
22. "Hey, wait a _____!"
23. Letter-shaped building wings
24. Part of PBS, for short
25. Math class with variables: abbr.
27. Emirate now home to the world's tallest skyscraper
29. Hirsute
31. Purchase
34. Mr. Hoggett's wife, in "Babe"
37. Scant
40. New Zealand yam
41. Café event where a cartoon mouse bares his soul?: 3 wds.
44. Beatty of Superman I and II
45. Peter of "The Lion in Winter"
46. General _____ chicken
47. Move like a whirlpool
49. String quartet member
51. Pre-toddler health problem

54. Type of booster shot, for short
55. "Mamma _____!" (hit musical)
58. The Buckeye State
60. Hall-of-Famer Ripken
62. Robert Pattinson, in "Twilight"
64. Horse relative from Mexico?: 2 wds.
67. Fired
68. Spam format
69. The munchies, e.g.
70. Riesling, for one
71. Tennis star Monica
72. In the ballpark
73. Part of ASL: abbr.

DOWN

1. Downhill racers
2. NBC morning show
3. Levels out
4. Wine list companion
5. It's set for some games: 2 wds.
6. Kanga's son, in "Winnie the Pooh"
7. Takes control of
8. Like a jaybird?
9. Dude
10. Make beloved
11. Finger food served with cheese and onions
12. Richard who played Jaws in James Bond movies
13. "Bloom County" penguin
19. Coin used before the euro

21. Sound from a lamb
26. _____-Roman wrestling
28. Natural ability
29. Coop dweller
30. "What a country!" comedian Smirnoff
32. Grand Canyon effect
33. Charlie Brown epithet
34. Seemingly forever
35. Gush forth
36. Of healing properties
38. Really, really cold
39. Shocking situation: 2 wds.
42. Gangster's girl
43. "Make _____ double"

48. Newcomer
50. Inc., overseas
52. Winter forecast
53. Justin Wilson's cooking style
55. General truth
56. Ryan who played Granny Clampett
57. One who combines
58. Pindaric poems
59. Away's opposite
61. Tackle box gadget
63. Baba _____ (Gilda Radner character on "Saturday Night Live")
65. Golfer Ernie
66. Title for a Khan

Answers on page 177.

GRID FILL

To complete this puzzle, place the given letters and words into the shapes in this grid. Words and letters will run across, down, and wrap around each shape. When the grid is filled, each row will contain one of the following words: bought, create, papers, savers, stream, thorny, tomato.

1. S, Y, E

2. MR, PC, PE

3. ATOM, BOAR, EARS, RATE, TOSS

4. TAVERN

5. THOUGHT

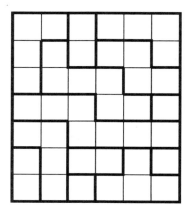

BLACK DIAMONDS

Place the numbers 1 through 4 in the cells of each of the squares below. There's a catch though: Overlapping squares must add up to the number given in each of the black diamonds.

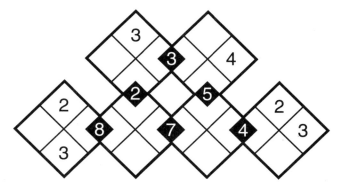

Answers on page 177.

FUTOSHIKI

Place the numbers 1 through 6 in each row and column. Numbers do not repeat in any row or column. Inequality restraints (less-than and greater-than symbols) must be met when placing numbers.

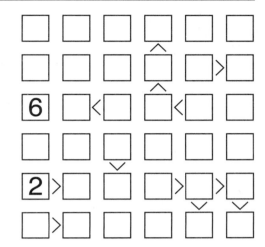

CALCU-DOKU

Use arithmetic and deductive logic to complete the grid so that each row and column contains the numbers 1 through 5 in some order. Numbers in each outlined set of squares combine to produce the number in the top corner using the mathematical sign indicated.

40×		3+		1-
	15×		10+	
8+	2			2/
	4+		12+	
8×				

Answers on page 177.

TANGLEWORDS

Think of this puzzle like a word search, only in reverse. Rather than finding the words in the grid, your job is to fill them in. Words begin only from the letters given in the shaded boxes and they appear in a straight line diagonally, horizontally, or vertically. They may appear backward or forward. When complete, every word will have been used, and the grid will have no empty squares.

ABACK

ABETTING

ACROSS

ALBATROSS

AMETHYST

ASCENDING

ATHLETIC

BACKTRACK

BLOCK

BREADTH

CAPTAIN

CIRCUIT

CREASED

DIRECTIVE

DISCIPLINE

DITCH

DURESS

GAUDIER

HAIRY

HATRED

ICES

KISSERS

LIMP

PATTERNS

PECAN

PETALS

PLEASES

POSSESS

PUSHES

RICHES

SCYTHES

SUBDIVISION

SUPERB

TALENTED

TALKATIVE

TARTAN

TULIP

UNAWARES

VERY

Answers on page 177.

L'ADDER

Starting at the bottom rung, use the numbers 1 through 9 to add up to the top number. Numbers can only be used once. The precise sums must be met along the way.

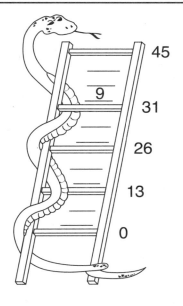

45

9

31

26

13

0

FILLOMINO

Fill in the grid with the numbers 1 through 8. Each number will be connected—horizontally or vertically—to a block of numbers all containing the same amount. So, a cell with the number 2 in it will be connected to another cell with the number 2; a cell with the number 3 will be connected to two more cells with the number 3.

	4		4		3	2	
	8		8	7		7	4
8			3		7		
				4	6			4
	1		2	1	8		6	
1			3	3				
			6			1			3
	6	6		6	8		2	
	8	6		3		1		

Answers on page 177.

3-D WORD SEARCH

This puzzle follows the rules of your typical word search: Every snake listed is contained within the group of letters. Words can be found in a straight line horizontally, vertically, or diagonally. But, in this version, words wrap up, down, and around the 3 sides of the cube.

ANACONDA

ASP

BOA CONSTRICTOR

BUSHMASTER

COTTONMOUTH

DIAMONDBACK

FER DE LANCE

GARTER

HOGNOSE

KING COBRA

KRAIT

MAMBA

MILK SNAKE

MOCCASIN

PUFF ADDER

PYTHON

RACER

RAT SNAKE

RATTLER

SIDEWINDER

VIPER

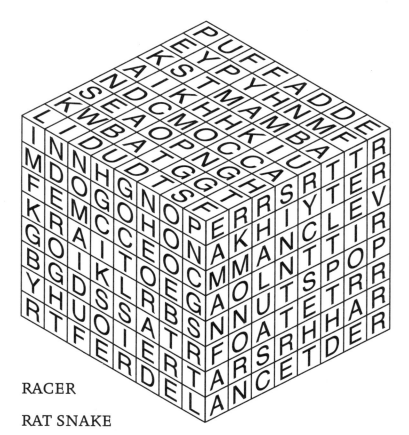

Answers on page 178.

ACROSS THE BOARD

Fill in the grid with a path of consecutive numbers starting at 1 and ending at 49. Numbers may connect vertically, horizontally, or diagonally.

	4		6		37	
29		①		35	39	
	30	32			41	
			9			
	24			14	44	
	18		15		13	
19		17			47	㊾

EVENS/ODDS

Arrange the numbers 2, 4, and 6 horizontally and vertically in groups of three. Similarly, arrange the numbers 1, 3, and 5 into groups of three. Combinations connect with one another on shared numbers (a vertical 135 can connect with a horizontal 513) and the even and odd numbers will intertwine.

2			■
■			3
2		6	
■	5		

Answers on page 178.

DIGITAL SUDOKU

Fill in the grid so that each row, column, and 2 by 3 block contains the numbers 1 through 6 exactly once. Numbers are in digital form and some segments have already been filled in.

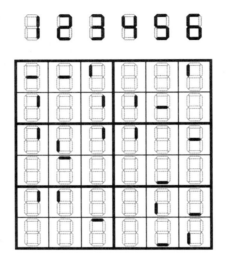

ADDAGRAM

This puzzle functions exactly like an anagram (a word that is a rearrangement of another word) with an added step: In addition to being scrambled, each word below is missing the same letter. Discover the missing letter and then unscramble the words. When you do, you'll reveal a color, a form of government, a record of historical events, and a word relating to atomic energy.

MINORS

HARMONY

CHLORINE

UNREAL

Answers on page 178.

ARROW WORD

This puzzle works exactly like a crossword, only the clues are embedded within the grid. Arrows point to the direction the clue applies, either across or down.

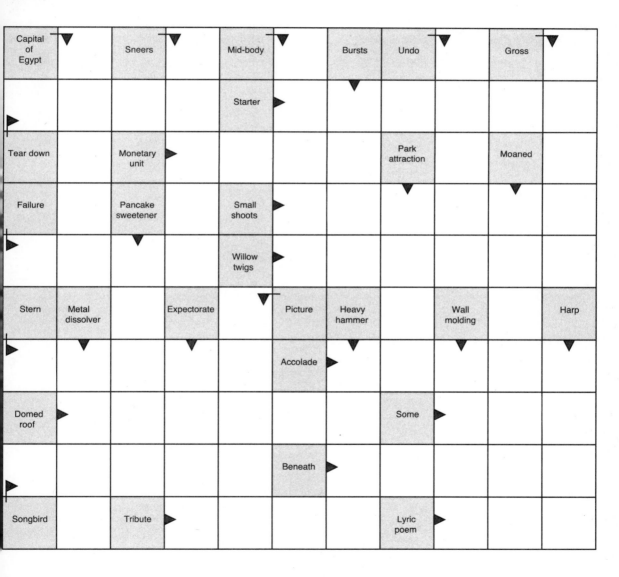

Answers on page 178.

MINESWEEPER

There are 12 mines hidden in the grid. Numbers indicate the amount of mines adjacent to that square, horizontally, vertically, and diagonally. We've entered one to get you started.

2	✸					1
	3	1			1	1
				1	1	
			1			
	3	2				1
1						
		1		4		1
	0				1	

SPLIT DECISIONS

Fill in each set of empty cells with letters that will create English words reading both across and down. Letters may repeat within a single set. We've completed one set to get you started.

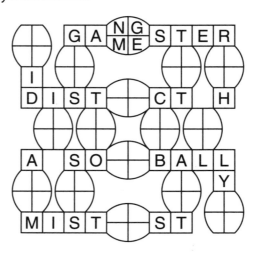

Answers on page 178.

HAMSTER TREADMILL

Which 2 of these exercise devices allows the hamster to run freely without the belts getting stuck? Is it device A, B, or C?

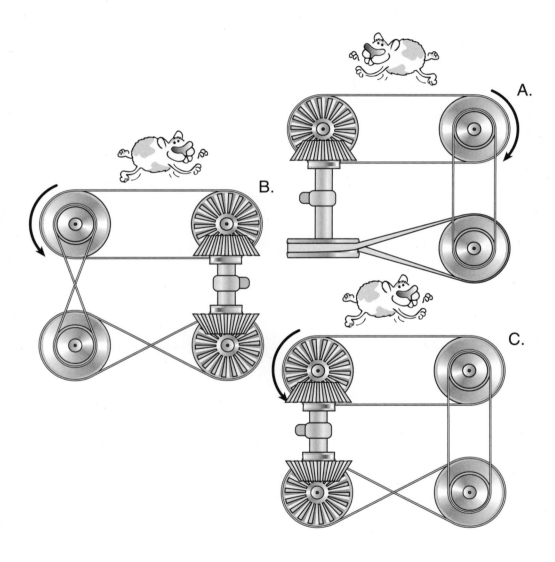

Answers on page 178.

ALL IN THE FAMILY

These talented families not only had brothers who played major-league ball, but these brothers all played for the same team at the same time. Names can be found in a straight line vertically, horizontally, or diagonally, and may read forward or backward. Leftover letters reveal other family same-team pairings.

AARON (Hank and Tommie)

ALLEN (Dick and Hank)

ALOMAR (Roberto and Sandy Jr.)

ALOU (Felipe, Jesus, and Matty)

BENES (Alan and Andy)

BIGBEE (Carson and Lyle)

BLANKENSHIP (Homer and Ted)

BOONE (Aaron and Bret)

BRETT (George and Ken)

CANSECO (Jose and Ozzie)

CONIGLIARO (Billy and Tony)

CRUZ (Hector, Jose, and Tommy)

DEAN (Dizzy and Paul)

GIAMBI (Jason and Jeremy)

GLAVINE (Mike and Tom)

GUERRERO (Vladimir and Wilton)

GWYNN (Chris and Tony)

MARTINEZ (Pedro and Ramon)

MATHEWSON (Christy and Henry)

NIEKRO (Joe and Phil)

PERRY (Jim and Gaylord)

REUSCHEL (Paul and Rick)

RIPKEN (Billy and Cal Jr.)

SEWELL (Joe and Luke)

TORRE (Frank and Joe)

WANER (Lloyd and Paul)

WEAVER (Jeff and Jered)

WHEAT (Mack and Zack)

WRIGHT (George, Harry, and Sam)

```
K E N G R L E H C S U E R A M O L A
D E A N O S W E H T A M Z I R F F E
P Y S A Y R R E P N D K U E E N G W
Z I R E I N O R A A I F R F E Y H J
E R H G W Y N N A V N R C T T E R B
N D H S T E I M R A E I N E A S I A
I T N D N T L I M U N R O T R R P A
T O S E N E B L G I O N E R E S K J
R R R W E R K E T H O L E N K O E N
A R G L A V I N E L B Y A L L E N F
M E A O C E S N A C T W H E R S I O
N T E A M O R A I L G I N O C M A N
T E S I N E E B G I B M A I G M L B
```

Leftover letters: _____

MATH CLASS

What is the value of -52 — -87?

Answers on page 179.

LOTUS MAZE

Help this flower bloom. Start at the seed at the top of the maze and help it grow by finding the path to the Lotus flower in the middle.

Answer on page 179.

CRACK THE CODE

The 4 symbols each represent a different number between 1 and 9. The numbers to the right and below the grid show the totals of that row or column. Can you deduce the numerical value of each symbol?

✳	✦	♣	☆	21
☆	♣	☆	✦	13
✦	✳	✦	✳	32
☆	✦	♣	☆	13
18	27	16	18	

PERFECT SCORE

Make 3 successful hits so that the sum of the numbers is 100. Double and triple scores do not apply. Numbers may be used more than once.

Answers on page 179.

ODD-EVEN LOGIDOKU

The numbers 1 through 9 appear once in every row, column, long diagonal, 3 by 3 grid, and irregular shape. Cells marked with the letter **E** contain even numbers. From the numbers already given, can you complete the puzzle?

SPELL MATH!

Spell out numbers in the blanks below to obtain the correct solution. Numbers are used only once and range from 1 to 20. Three letters have been given to get you started.

S ___ ___ + ___ h ___ ___ ___ = ___ i ___ ___

Answers on page 179.

WHAT'S ON?

The letters in BECKER can be found in boxes 6, 15, 18, 19, and 25 but not necessarily in that order. Similarly, the letters in all the other TV shows can be found in the boxes indicated. Your task is to insert all the letters of the alphabet into the boxes. If you do this correctly, the shaded cells will reveal what these shows have in common.

Hint: Compare FRASIER and PARIS to get the value of **P**, then PARIS to MAVERICK for the value of **S**.

1	2	3	4	5	6	7	8	9	10	11	12	13
14	15	16	17	18	19	20	21	22	23	24	25	26
												Q

Unused letter: Q

BECKER: 6, 15, 18, 19, 25

COLUMBO: 5, 14, 15, 16, 23, 25

FRASIER: 4, 6, 7, 11, 18, 24

GIDGET: 1, 6, 8, 11, 12

HAZEL: 4, 6, 10, 17, 23

KOJAK: 4, 14, 19, 20

MANNIX: 3, 4, 5, 9, 11

MATLOCK: 1, 4, 5, 14, 15, 19, 23

MAUDE: 4, 5, 6, 12, 16

MAVERICK: 2, 4, 5, 6, 11, 15, 18, 19

NEWHART: 1, 3, 4, 6, 17, 18, 21

PARIS: 4, 7, 11, 13, 18

PHYLLIS: 7, 11, 13, 17, 22, 23

ROSEANNE: 3, 4, 6, 7, 14, 18

SEINFELD: 3, 6, 7, 11, 12, 23, 24

Answers on page 179.

One detail is missing from each soldier. Can you find which detail is missing in each?

Answers on page 179.

WORD COLUMNS

Find the hidden quote from Dr. Martin Luther King Jr. by using the letters directly below each of the blank squares. Each letter is used only once. A black square indicates the end of a word.

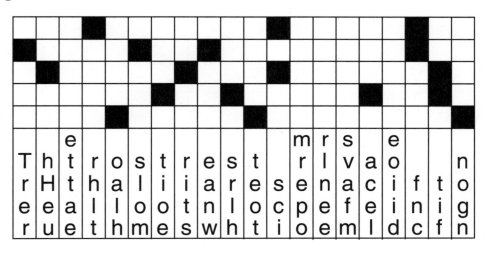

VEX-A-GON

Place the numbers 1 through 6 into the triangles of each hexagon. The numbers may be in any order, but they do not repeat within each hexagon shape.

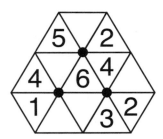

Answers on page 179.

DOUBLED UP

This puzzle works exactly like a crossword, except instead of placing one letter in each box, you place 2. Words are written across in each box. As a bonus, unscramble the 10 letters found in the shaded boxes to answer the definition below.

ACROSS

1. Assess
5. Higher-up
6. Type of tuna
8. Tiny matter
10. Bullfighter
11. Earmarked

DOWN

2. Force
3. Irregular, random
4. Long-neck onion
7. Hairdo
8. Rural
9. Gave a speech

Like stormy, windy weather: _____

Answers on page 180.

LOGINUMBER

Determine the values of the letters below using 2 rules: Each letter is no greater than the number of letters in the puzzle; none of the letters are equal to each other.

Use the grid to help keep track of possible solutions.

E + B > A

H + B = 5

D + G = 9

E + H = G

D + 1 = C

	1	2	3	4	5	6	7	8
A								
B								
C								
D								
E								
F								
G								
H								

WORD SUMS

In the addition problem below, each letter represents a number between 0 and 9. Decipher the letters to reach a correct numerical conclusion.

```
    S O L V E
    S O L V E
    S O L V E
  + S O L V E
    G A M E S
```

Answers on page 180.

CRACK THE CODE

The 7 symbols each represent a different number between 1 and 10. The numbers to the right and below the grid show the totals of that row or column. Can you deduce the numerical value of each symbol?

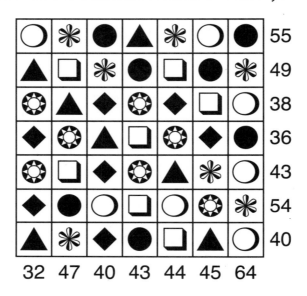

55
49
38
36
43
54
40

32 47 40 43 44 45 64

OPPOSITES

Use the letters below to fill in the boxes and reveal the 2 related words. Connected boxes share the same letter.

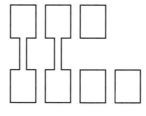

AENWX

Answers on page 180.

BATTLE BOATS

Place each ship in the fleet located at right within the grid. Ships may be placed horizontally or vertically, but they don't touch each other, not even diagonally. Numbers reveal the ship segments located in that row or column. Two submarines have been added to get you started.

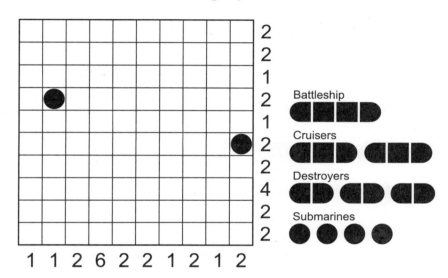

BLACK DIAMONDS

Place the numbers 1 through 4 in the cells of each of the squares at right. There's a catch though: Overlapping squares must add up to the number given in each of the black diamonds.

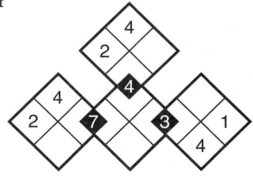

Answers on page 180.

KITCHEN UTENSILS

ACROSS

1. Have a strong desire for
6. Part of a slalom path
9. Progressive Insurance spokeswoman
12. "Bleeding Love" singer Leona
13. "The light dawns!"
14. Flush out, with "of"
15. Horseshoe-shaped fastener
16. "Everybody Loves _____"
18. Utensil used for beating egg whites: 2 wds.
20. "Star Wars" nickname
21. Sweater sticker?
22. Geisha's belt
25. "Models _____" (1990s TV show)
27. They may be essential
30. Utensil used for flipping flapjacks: 2 wds.
34. RPM dial
35. Call yours
36. Metro maker
37. Shopper's notes
40. Belief system
42. Food-gripping utensils: 2 wds.
47. Temporary camp
48. Tabriz native
49. Had a burger
50. Gun letters
51. Jay's successor, temporarily
52. HRH part
53. "Jungle Book" python
54. Works on a necktie

DOWN

1. Word after book or country
2. Sitcom starring a country singer
3. Hunted by MPs, perhaps
4. Country house

5. Olympic skater Maria Sergiejeva's country
6. Make money
7. Head and shoulders protection
8. Greet cordially: 2 wds.
9. Cupcake topper
10. "You are the weakest _____!"
11. Unusual
17. Not an adult
19. Pig noise
22. Pull (out)
23. Sheep noise
24. Doing very well moneywise: 2 wds.
26. Maureen Chiquet, at Chanel

28. Bruce or Brenda
29. Like well-attended concerts: abbr.
31. One of the Marx Brothers
32. MAC _____ lipstick
33. Loosen
38. Pepe Le Pew is one
39. Pageant queen's headwear
41. Idiot
42. Low-cal
43. College sports inits.
44. iPod variety
45. Tiny swarmer
46. There are 7 deadly ones
47. "Foiled again!"

PRAY, BUT KEEP YOUR EYES OPEN

Cryptograms are messages in substitution code. Break the code to read the quote and its author. For example, THE SMART CAT might become FVO QWGDF JGF if **F** is substituted for **T**, **V** for **H**, **O** for **E**, and so on.

"DJOW QJO LTIITYWHCTOI NHLO QY HMCTNH
QJOP JHK QJO ATAUO HWK DO JHK QJO UHWK.
QJOP IHTK, 'UOQ XI VCHP.' DO NUYIOK YXC
OPOI. DJOW DO YVOWOK QJOL DO JHK QJO
ATAUO HWK QJOP JHK QJO UHWK."

—ATIJYV KOILYWK QXQX

Answers on page 180.

NUMBER SEARCH

Every number set listed is contained within the group of numbers below. Number sets can be found in a straight line horizontally, vertically, or diagonally. They may read either backward or forward.

01902	35426
03241	36718
04440	37700
05050	38716
06789	39901
08909	40004
09910	42510
12345	48480
13928	49012
16161	50505
17280	52901
20192	53535
21092	54098
23091	55431
25543	57821
26718	59012
28901	61010
30003	62312
31902	63333
32323	64646
33410	65009

```
2 2 5 6 7 3 2 2 7 9 8 1 7 6 3
0 6 1 8 9 8 1 2 0 9 8 1 7 6 2
1 0 9 8 2 7 9 0 8 1 2 1 0 9 5
9 5 7 8 2 1 5 6 2 1 6 7 6 1 2
8 6 4 6 4 6 3 9 7 5 6 7 6 6 9
0 7 1 0 2 3 4 4 1 2 3 0 9 1 0
8 8 3 0 5 0 5 0 5 3 0 5 2 6 1
2 9 9 9 1 1 4 1 4 5 8 9 3 1 1
9 1 3 0 0 0 3 4 8 4 8 0 1 5 8
0 8 3 4 9 6 2 3 1 2 4 0 9 3 7
1 0 9 9 3 9 1 5 1 6 8 0 0 7 6
2 9 1 0 2 4 5 4 5 4 6 7 0 3 5
0 0 0 1 4 8 6 7 1 0 2 7 3 0 4
2 9 8 2 5 5 4 3 2 3 2 3 8 0 4
4 6 5 8 3 4 1 0 1 4 3 3 0 9 8
```

66789	73344	83410	92319
67612	74510	85855	93434
68886	75676	86710	94010
69090	77111	87654	96720
71023	80076	89102	98765
72237	81209	91085	99911

Answers on page 180.

GET IT STRAIGHT

Don't get too caught up in all the twists and turns as you negotiate your way to the center of this cowboy labyrinth.

ADDAGRAM

This puzzle functions exactly like an anagram (a word that is a rearrangement of another word) with an added step: In addition to being scrambled, each word below is missing the same letter. Discover the missing letter and then unscramble the words. When you do, you'll reveal a French dish, a surgical tool, a noise that gradually gets louder, and a radical decision.

STORAGE

LAPELS

CENSORED

TRIADS

Answers on pages 180–181.

EVENS/ODDS

Arrange the numbers 2, 4, and 6 horizontally and vertically in groups of three. Similarly, arrange the numbers 1, 3, and 5 into groups of three. Combinations connect with one another on shared numbers (a vertical 135 can connect with a horizontal 513) and the even and odd numbers will intertwine.

KLUMP

Shade in some of the numbers so the remaining connected sets of numbers match the following sums:

1, 8, 10, 13, 18, 20

A solitary number (not connected to any other) can represent one or more of these sums.

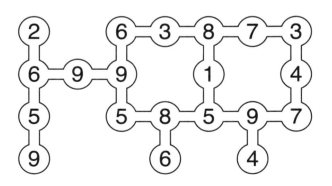

Answers on page 181.

FIFTEEN UP

Divide the grid into 15 regions. The sum of each region must be 15. Numbers are used only once.

10	2	3	7	3	2	8
2	2	8	6	5	3	2
1	9	2	11	3	1	7
2	6	4	4	2	10	3
7	6	1	3	2	1	5
6	5	3	12	3	5	10
1	5	2	7	1	7	5

CROSS SUMS

Use the numbers below to fill in the grid. Each cell at the top of the 3 adjacent cells is the sum of numbers below it. So, as seen in the example, A=B+C+D. Here's the numbers needed to fill in the bottom 2 rows:

1 2 3 4 5 6 6 7 12 15 18

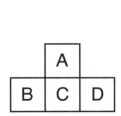

Answers on page 181.

LITERARY SEARCH

Can you find the 8 popular book titles depicted in this illustration?

TRIVIA ON THE BRAIN
Each year, teams of college students compete in the Brain Bowl, during which they answer questions in 5 categories: neuroanatomy, neurochemistry, neurophysiology, brain and behavior, and drugs and the brain.

Answers on page 181.

SUM FUN

In this grid, there are 30 instances where the sum of 31 can be obtained by adding numbers in a vertical, horizontal, or diagonal direction. Find and circle them all.

```
2 2 8 4 3 4 2 7 8 7
7 5 7 5 9 8 6 3 6 9
5 2 9 5 9 8 4 3 1 6
2 6 2 9 8 9 1 5 5 3
8 5 8 3 3 2 8 3 7 2
7 8 5 8 5 2 8 7 1 4
9 8 7 9 7 1 7 4 6 7
4 6 3 6 7 3 7 7 7 5
8 2 8 1 1 6 8 1 6 3
1 2 8 6 9 7 3 4 7 6
```

MINESWEEPER

There are 25 mines hidden in the grid. Numbers indicate the amount of mines adjacent to that square, horizontally, vertically, and diagonally. We've entered one to get you started.

1			1			1			1
				1	1		2		
	2								
1			3	3		4	1		1
								1	
		1			1			2	
1			3			3			1
	1					2			
					1		2		
1	✸	2	1			1			1

Answers on page 181.

ARROW WORD

This puzzle works exactly like a crossword, only the clues are embedded within the grid. Arrows point to the direction the clue applies, either across or down.

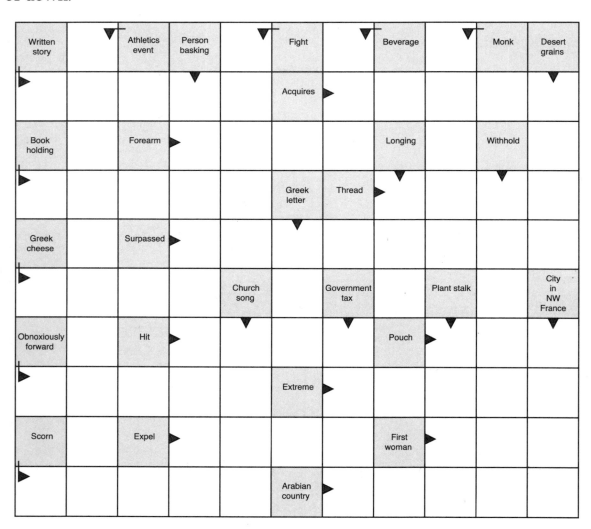

Answers on page 181.

SPLIT DECISIONS

Fill in each set of empty cells with letters that will create English words reading both across and down. Letters may repeat within a single set. We've completed one set to get you started.

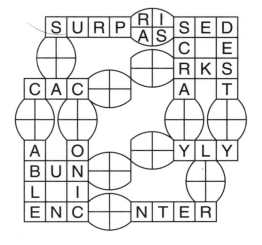

HITORI

The object of this puzzle is to have a number appear only once in each row and column. By shading a number cell, you are effectively removing that number from its row and column. There's a catch though: Shaded number cells are never adjacent to one another in a row or column.

3	1	8	9	6	6	2
8	9	6	1	6	6	3
1	6	5	8	3	8	6
5	3	6	8	1	1	5
3	5	2	8	8	9	5
6	2	6	5	1	9	8
9	6	3	6	1	2	1

Answers on pages 181–182.

KAKURO

Place a number from 1 through 9 in each empty cell so that the sum of each vertical or horizontal run (rows and columns extending from already numbered cells) equals the number at the top or on the left of that run. Numbers may not be repeated in any run, and runs end at dark-colored squares.

SPELL MATH!

Spell out numbers in the blanks below to obtain the correct solution. Numbers are used only once and range from 1 to 20. A letter has been given to get you started.

___ ___ ___ ___ + f ___ ___ ___ ___ ___ ___ = ___ ___ ___ ___ ___ ___

Answers on page 182.

RED, WHITE, BLUE, AND GREEN

Each row, column, and long diagonal contains 2 reds, 2 whites, 2 blues, and 2 greens. From the clues given below, can you complete the grid?

1. Each blue is immediately left of each green.

2. Two whites, a red, and a blue are directly enclosed by both the greens.

3. The greens are separated by 5 cells; the whites are adjacent.

4. No clue needed.

5. No clue needed.

6. The pattern of colors takes the form abcbdcad.

7. Two whites, a red, and a blue are directly enclosed by both the greens.

8. Two blues, 2 greens, and a red are directly enclosed by both the whites.

A. A green is directly enclosed by both the reds.

B. Two blues and a green are directly enclosed by both the whites.

C. No clue needed.

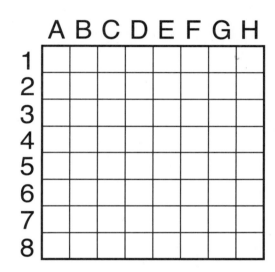

D. No clue needed.

E. Each green is directly above each blue.

F. Both the greens are directly enclosed by a blue and a red.

G. The blues are adjacent.

H. The reds cannot be found in cells 5, 6, 7, or 8; 3 different colors are directly enclosed by both the blues.

Answer on page 182.

WORD SPIRAL

This puzzle works exactly like a crossword, only without the divisions between words. In fact, some words blend into one another, so solving one clue will help you solve another. Numbers indicate the boxes answers occupy.

1-4. Harbor

1-7. Act as

5-9. Manmade fabric

7-12. Off at a distance

10-15. Establish by deduction

12-18. Certain steelworker

14-20. Long-time pro

18-23. Feeling of ill-will

21-27. Amiable

24-29. Actors' lines (var.)

27-32. Stoppage

30-37. Gala affair

33-36. Gun barrel diameter

35-41. Vote back in

37-44. Galvanic

42-47. More wealthy

45-50. Recluse

48-54. Winter hand-warmers

51-55. On edge

1	2	3	4	5	6	7	8	9
32	33	34	35	36	37	38	39	10
31	56	57	58	59	60	61	40	11
30	55	72	73	74	75	62	41	12
29	54	71	80		76	63	42	13
28	53	70	79	78	77	64	43	14
27	52	69	68	67	66	65	44	15
26	51	50	49	48	47	46	45	16
25	24	23	22	21	20	19	18	17

54-59. Tranquil

57-61. Foe

60-63. Legendary tale

62-67. Prevent

64-70. African wild swine

68-74. Baloney

71-76. Laundry appliance

75-80. Shorttail weasel

77-80. Planted bomb

Answers on page 182.

CALCU-DOKU

Use arithmetic and deductive logic to complete the grid so that each row and column contains the numbers 1 through 4 in some order. Numbers in each outlined set of squares combine to produce the number in the top corner using the mathematical sign indicated.

3×		6+	
6×	2−		5+
	8×		
6+		2−	

NEIGHBORHOOD

Place the numbers 1 through 6 in the circles below. For each number, the sum of all the numbers connected to it is given. Numbers can only be used once.

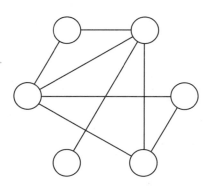

1 = 13

2 = 16

3 = 5

4 = 7

5 = 10

6 = 3

Answers on page 182.

CROSS SUMS

Use the numbers below to fill in the grid. Each cell at the top of a cross is the sum of numbers below it. So, as seen in the example, A=B+C+D+E.

1 2 3 4 5 6 7 9 10 11 37 44 46

54 85 118 161 329 408 1316

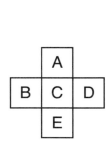

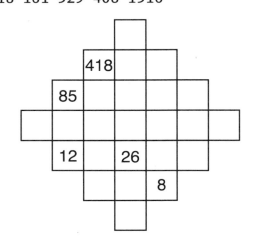

MASTERMIND

The goal of this puzzle is to replace the question marks with a correct sequence of numbers. The numbers you need for the answer are contained in the rows above the question marks. Follow these 2 guides: A black dot indicates that a number needed for the solution is in that row and in the correct position; a white dot means that a number needed for the solution is in that row but in the wrong position. Numbers do not appear more than once in the solution, and the solution never begins with 0.

Answers on page 182.

STAR POWER

Fill in each of the empty squares in the grid so that each star is surrounded by the numbers 1 through 8 with no repeats.

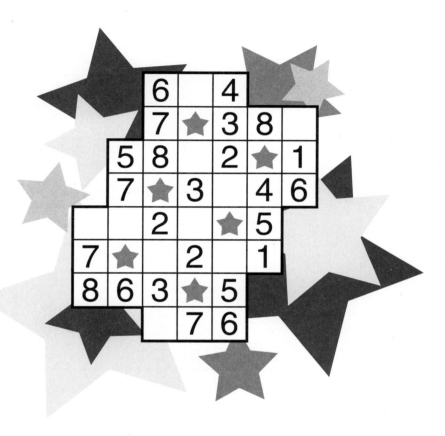

TRIVIA ON THE BRAIN
The brain is only 3 percent of the total weight of the body, but it uses a whopping 17 percent of the body's energy.

Answer on page 182.

CHAIN SUDOKU

Use deductive logic to complete the grid so that each row, each column, and each connected set of circles contains the numbers 1 through 5 in some order. The solution is unique.

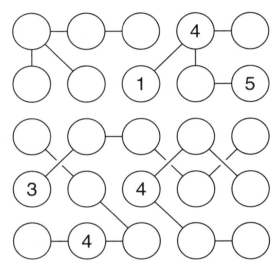

OPPOSITES

Use the letters below to fill in the boxes and reveal the 2 related words. Connected boxes share the same letter.

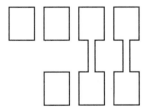

AEFNR

Answers on page 182.

PUBLISHING POETRY

Palindrome Press has 5 new poetry books coming out this year, and they've had to bring on several new editors to ensure that each book makes its intended launch date. Each book has a different author, and each has been assigned to a different editor to get the manuscript ready for publication. Using only the clues below, match each book to its author and editor, and determine the month in which each book is scheduled to be published.

1. Valerie isn't the editor assigned to Fanny Farnsworth's new book (which isn't titled "Thieves City").

Months	Authors	Titles	Editors
August			
September			
October			
November			
December			

2. Of "For Gerald" and "Driven Away," one was written by Betty Beaufort and the other is scheduled for a September launch.

3. Between "Nine Takes" and the book Jeff is editing, one will be released in November and the other was written by Dorothy Dickens.

4. Of "Thieves City" and the newest book by Penny Pennington, one will be the last of the 5 to be published and the other has been assigned to Marilyn for editing.

5. The book Timothy is editing will be released one month after "Driven Away."

6. "California" (which isn't being edited by Marilyn) will be launched sometime before "Thieves City" and sometime after August.

7. "For Gerald" (which wasn't written by Betty Beaufort) will be released sometime before the book that Timothy is editing.

Answer on page 183.

FITTING WORDS

In this miniature crossword, the clues are listed randomly and are numbered for convenience only. It is up to you to figure out the placement of the 9 answers. To help you, we've inserted one letter in the grid, and this is the only occurrence of that letter in the completed puzzle.

CLUES

1. Leaves' home?

2. Narcissus adorer

3. Bellyache

4. Come about

5. Cry of pain

6. Mountain getaway

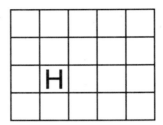

7. Matzo's lack

8. Battery fluid

9. "Song _____ Blue" (Neil Diamond hit)

1-2-3

Place the numbers 1, 2, or 3 in the empty circles. The challenge is to have only these 3 numbers in each connected row and column—no number should repeat. Any combination is allowed.

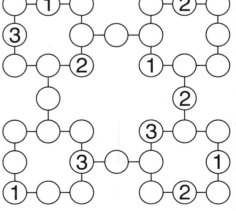

Answers on page 183.

Starting at the top left corner, place all the numbers as a continuous chain. The last digit of one number is the first digit of the following number.

06914

07583

09863

10021

19855

24856

31037

36194

36459

40264

47112

47721

57980

62440

74518

89210

94320

99919

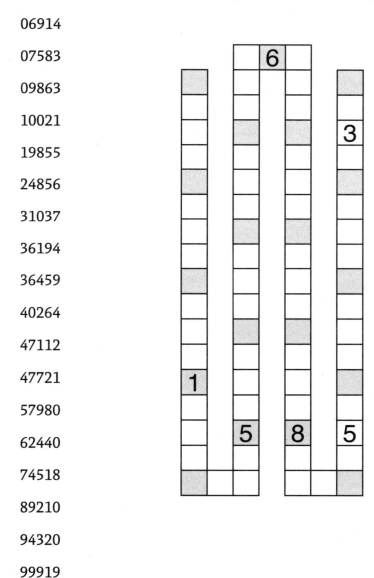

Answer on page 183.

DOUBLED UP

This puzzle works exactly like a crossword, except instead of placing one letter in each box, you place 2. Words are written across in each box. As a bonus, unscramble the 10 letters found in the shaded boxes to answer the definition below.

ACROSS
1. Birthplace
5. Applause
6. Memorial
8. Cabbage family vegetable
10. Shell-like instrument
11. Union member

DOWN
2. Dealer, trader
3. A city in Mexico
4. Next day
7. Untidiest
8. Girl with dark hair
9. Radio audience

Hodgepodge: _____

Answers on page 183.

STARSTRUCK

Journey from Earth (E) to Mars (Ma), hitting all the other planets along the way. Keep track of the days it takes to travel between planets using the empty boxes below.

If you are able to make the trip in 25 or more days, you are a Promising Pilot; less than 22 days, a Nifty Navigator; less than 18 days, an Amazing Astronaut; do it in 14 days, and you'll be a Master of the Universe!

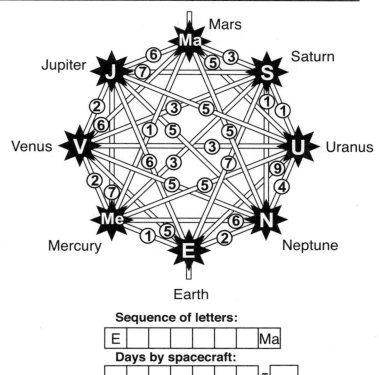

Sequence of letters:

E							Ma

Days by spacecraft:

								=	

FILLOMINO

Fill in the grid with the numbers 1 through 4. Each number will be connected—horizontally or vertically—to a block of numbers all containing the same amount. So a cell with the number 2 in it will be connected to another cell with the number 2; a cell with the number 3 will be connected to two more cells with the number 3.

	1		4
			3
2			1
3			
2		3	

Answers on page 183.

DOMESTIC LOGIC

On Box Street, there are 5 adjacent houses that are identical to each other. You've been asked to visit Mr. Stark, but without any addresses on the doors you are not sure which house to approach. At the local coffee shop, you ask the waitress for help. She is able to provide the following information:

A. There are always decorations in House B's windows and in one of the houses adjacent to it.

B. Mr. Stark hates decorations.

C. The occupants of House E keep to themselves.

D. Mr. Stark's girlfriend lives in House C, but they don't live together.

E. Mr. Stark and his girlfriend think alike in all regards.

Where does Mr. Stark live?

WORD JIGSAW

Fit the pieces into the frame to form common words reading across and down. There's no need to rotate the pieces; they'll fit as shown, with each piece used once.

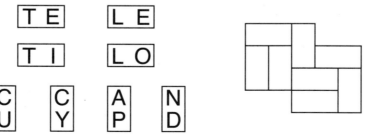

Answers on page 183.

SUDOKU

Use deductive logic to complete the grid so that each row, each column, and each 3 by 3 box contains the numbers 1 through 9 in some order. The solution is unique.

7		6			4			8
	1	4			5		6	
5	2		6	9		7		
	6	1		4	2			
		7				1		
			9	1		4	7	
		2		8	9		4	3
	5		2			8	9	
6			4			5		7

WORD SUMS

In the addition problem below, each letter represents a number between 0 and 9. Decipher the letters to reach a correct numerical conclusion.

```
   B E L L
+  G O N G
---------
 B A N J O
```

Answers on page 183.

SHROUDED SUMMARY

Hidden in the word search is a summary of a well-known novel. The words you need to find are listed below; in the word search they are presented in an order that makes more sense. The words may be vertical, horizontal, or diagonal. As a bonus, can you name the novel and its author?

AND

ASSUMES

CON MAN

DISCOVERY

FEARING

FOREVER

FRIEND

HIS

IDENTITY

MURDERS

STRUGGLING

WEALTHY

YOUNG

```
S D N L Y F E R N G J I S T R L O
V T M C O N M A N A S M O E S K L
F R R I U N D U I H E N I T D Y K
W E T U N A L T R H Y C N O M N A
F O E R G V E R E D M U D D V E R
R D E R D G Y O G W E A L T H Y U
D I C S V O L R Y S F R I E N D C
F I D N T H F I O L L W S I A N D
N G W R O D S A N N O E T T S H W
O R D W H P P E I G N W H I S O R
D S E H C R N S O I E R O D U I D
U T E O D I V C R O C Y T E M K O
S T R W N K L A N F U S T N E R O
I D P Z L S R A N O I N G T S F R
M I B R N I A W H L B E N I E F T
C O M R P A E N S O S K L T I L D
E W R T I E R C N A B H U Y G E C
O N S E Q E U F O R E V E R N C E
S B A L Y D W O E R D F D L E S R
S E D I S A T S E A R U S O R E M
E M B D I S C O V E R Y B E R R E
A D E R S T P O A T T I E N N O I
T P A R I T U C L R A F N D I E D
A M A G F I N C I D L Q B G C L I
```

Novel and author: _____

Answers on page 184.

CHAIN GRID FILL

To complete this puzzle, place the words into the chains in this grid. Words will run across, down, and diagonally around each chain. When the grid is complete, each column will contain one of the following words: barefoot, bottle, burger, coffee, download, drinks, maintain, market, mountain, scully, Spartans. We filled in one word to get you started.

1. BAM, COD, DAY, SIN, TIN, TOE

2. NULL, RANK, TALE, TANK, TOWS

3. BARGE, PRINT

WATER TANKS

Each cubic tank holds 6 gallons of water. Fill in some of the tanks with water to satisfy the volume given in the rows and columns. Equilibrium must be met within each outlined set of tanks. Note that some tanks in rows or columns without specified amounts may be filled to meet this need.

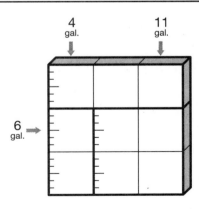

Answers on page 184.

ODD-EVEN LOGIDOKU

The numbers 1 through 9 appear once in every row, column, long diagonal, 3 by 3 grid, and irregular shape. Cells marked with the letter **E** contain even numbers. From the numbers already given, can you complete the puzzle?

FRAME GAMES™

Can you "read" the phrase below?

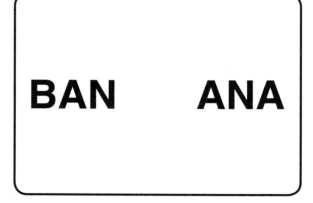

BAN   ANA

Answers on page 184.

HASHI

Each circle represents an island, with the number inside indicating the number of bridges connected to it. Draw bridges between islands using the number given. There can be no more than 2 bridges going in the same direction, and there must be a continuous path connecting all islands. Bridges can only be vertical or horizontal and may not cross islands or other bridges. We've drawn some bridges to get you started.

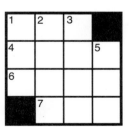

NUMBER CROSSWORD

Fill in this crossword with numbers instead of letters. Use the clues to determine which number from 1 through 9 belongs in each square. No zeros are used.

ACROSS

1. Consecutive digits, ascending
4. Consecutive digits, descending
6. A number of the form aabb
7. The sum of its digits is 14

DOWN

1. Consecutive digits, descending
2. A number of the form abba

3. The sum of its digits is 20
5. Consecutive digits, descending

Answers on page 184.

CODEWORD

The letters of the alphabet are hidden in code: They are represented by a random number from 1 through 26. With the letters already given, complete the crossword puzzle with English words and break the code.

9		18		17			17		21		10
26	20	6	10	10	14	17	3	24	9	4	19
26		7		19		17	24		2		17
9	25	9	16	15	17	21	19	13	19	15	21
23		15		21		6	9		17		17
20	16	20	14		17	22	9	20	10		
19		14		22		8		17		21		25
		22	5	16	4	10		23	19	21	9
12		10		16		6		17		1		11
6	20	16	13	19		6	24	21	20	16	15	19
24		2		26		7		24		6		20
17	18	16	4	20	17		24	15	26	24	4	20
21		19		14			25		17		19

A B C D E F G H I J K L M N O P Q R S T U V W X Y Z

1	2	3	4	5	6	7	8	9	10	11	12	13

14	15	16	17	18	19	20	21	22	23	24	25	26
Y						L						

Answer on page 184.

TIMES SQUARE

Fill in each empty cell of the grid with a number between 1 and 9. The product (multiplication) of the numbers in each row must be the value to the right of that row of the grid, and the product of each column must be the value below that column of the grid.

Important: The number 1 can only be used once in any row or column; other numbers can be repeated.

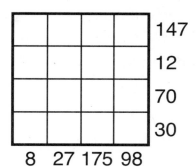

WORD LADDER

Use the clues to change just one letter on each line to go from the top word to the bottom word. Do not change the order of the letters. You must have a common English word at each step.

BRAIN

_____ down which water runs

_____ sketched by hand

_____ die in water

_____ to look down

FLOWN

Answers on page 185.

CROSS SCAN

Think of this puzzle as a crossword/word search hybrid. Answer each of the clues (numbers in parentheses indicate the numbers of letters in the answer), and then find the word in the letter grid on the next page. If you get stumped, scan the letter grid for words, and try to see if they match the clues.

This puzzle also has a hidden theme, which will be revealed as you get closer to completion. Leftover letters spell out a saying that ties in with the theme.

1. Architect Christopher (4)

2. Peace symbol (4)

3. Stringed flyer (4)

4. Fence part (4)

5. Croon (4)

6. Fly aloft (4)

7. Envelope part (4)

8. Ova (4)

9. Home (4)

10. Toot horn (4)

11. Coat rack (4)

12. Payment due (4)

13. Large nose (4)

14. Sell (4)

15. Lady _____ Johnson (4)

16. Poe naysayer (5)

17. Scout rank (5)

18. Speedy (5)

19. Avian sound (5)

20. Ponder over (5)

21. McCartney band (5)

22. Sit (5)

23. Complain (6)

24. Old Ford model (6)

25. Glance (6)

26. Middle East country (6)

27. President Van Buren (6)

28. Clock alarm (6)

29. Set of stairs (6)

30. Laugh wildly (6)

B I N E R S N O E G I P H R T
S R E H T A E F D L R A O S F
S R V E F A F A F I E A N H I
T R A T L E T L H A D H K C W
H E R A U A A C E R N I W R S
G N Y B T P G O U D A V R E E
I C E U T S E N I U G N E P S
L A K C E E N I I N T L N W U
F R R N R E O T R T G S I E O
S D U I R V H R K A H N G N R
K I T K C O C A E P G G B O G
I N N F T D E M W S S R I W I
T A T G T B I R D K O E L N R
E L K C A C U C K O O I L N G
M I G R A T E G D I R T R A P

31. Vain person (7)

32. Antarctic resident (7)

33. Flurry (7)

34. Move (7)

35. Message carriers (7)

36. Church official (8)

37. Hatch eggs (8)

38. Duster material (8)

39. Singing TV family (9)

40. Young bird (9)

41. Coyote nemesis (10)

42. Nurse Florence (11)

Leftover letters: _____

Theme: _____

Answers on page 185.

FUTOSHIKI

Place the numbers 1 through 5 in each row and column. Numbers do not repeat in any row or column. Inequality restraints (less-than and greater-than symbols) must be met when placing numbers.

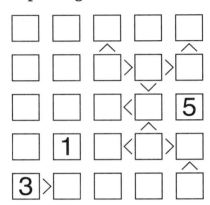

OPPOSITES

Use the letters below to fill in the boxes and reveal the 2 related words. Connected boxes share the same letter.

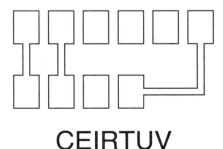

CEIRTUV

Answers on page 185.

ARROW WORD

This puzzle works exactly like a cross-word, only the clues are embedded within the grid. Arrows point to the direction the clue applies, either across or down.

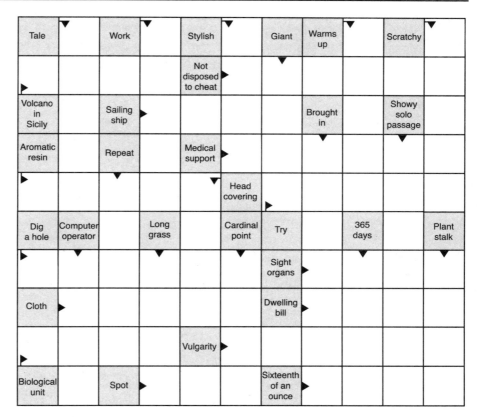

WORD SUMS

In the addition problem below, each letter represents a number between 0 and 9. Decipher the letters to reach a correct numerical conclusion.

```
    I R O N
+ X E N O N
R A D I U M
```

Answers on page 185.

SLITHERLINK PATH

Create a single continuous path along the dotted lines. The path does not cross itself or touch at any corners. Numbers indicate how many line segments surround each cell. We've filled in some line segments to get you started.

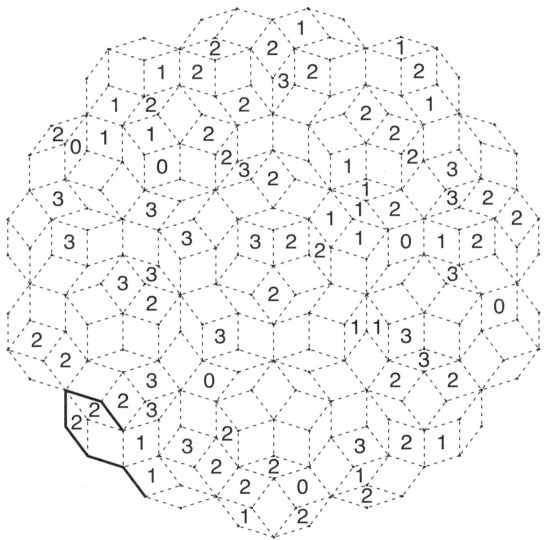

Answer on page 185.

BLACK DIAMONDS

Place the numbers 1 through 4 in the cells of each of the squares below. There's a catch though: Overlapping squares must add up to the number given in each of the black diamonds.

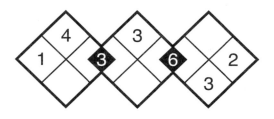

MARBLES

Place 12 marbles into the grid without having any touch one another, not even diagonally. There are some walls, represented by thick lines, that block the view of the marbles. Marbles must not "see" each other in a horizontal or vertical direction. We've placed one to get you started.

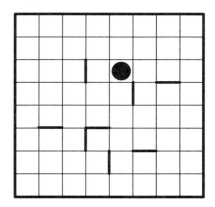

Answers on pages 185–186.

ROUND AND ROUND

ACROSS

1. Kind of rock music for David Bowie in the '70s
5. Where students sleep
9. Violinist Zimbalist
14. The Beatles' meter maid
15. It's often twisted apart
16. Director Sam
17. "No help needed": 2 wds.
18. Drive leisurely
20. Not really remembering what happened, say
22. They share 58-Across
23. "Yes, sailor"
25. Sheltered areas
26. Hippie's slogan: 2 wds.
30. When doubled, a dance
33. Sci-fi movie hero
34. Knighted actor McKellen
35. Mess up, as an evildoer's plans
36. Miners' quests
37. Word following the ends of this puzzle's four longest entries
40. Microsoft Word function
41. _____ IRA
42. Olive in the comics
43. Paradise lost
44. Put down, in the 'hood
45. Easily related to, as a TV show: 3 wds.
49. Put off

50. Alternative to caffeine for the tired
51. "101 Dalmatians" villain
54. Drink thirstily
58. What the lead gets: 2 wds.
62. Golda of Israel
63. Famed French sculptor
64. Machu Picchu constructor
65. Teri of "Meet the Parents"
66. Struck down, Biblically
67. Early Biblical figure
68. Wrench in the gears

DOWN

1. You're filling it right now
2. Peruvian capital
3. Comprehensive: 3 wds.
4. Urging to the birthday child: 3 wds.
5. Follow persistently
6. Spanish treasure
7. Frequent target of fans' vitriol
8. Farm animal, to kids: 2 wds.
9. Golf pencil's lack
10. Goes on a hunger strike
11. Philbin's cohost
12. Arab bigwig
13. 60-second units: abbr.
19. Karl of the Bush administration
21. Salon job
24. Clapton on the guitar
25. Devise
26. Norwegian attraction

27. The king of France
28. Playwright Clifford
29. Reward
30. Rice of the Bush admin.
31. Like many TVs nowadays
32. Stranded
35. Things often squeezed on road trips: 2 wds.
38. Strong substance
39. North Carolina school
45. Kind of solution for contact lenses
46. Boring time for employees

47. Bad way to be caught: 3 wds.
48. Website section for newbies: abbr.
49. _____ card
51. Middles: abbr.
52. 5-Across or 59-Down unit
53. Salon job
55. How long a wait might seem to last
56. Nike rival
57. Hopper
59. Stopover on a road trip
60. Sgt. or cpl.: abbr.
61. It comes out of 35-Down

Answers on page 186.

GOLF

Line up the putt to get a hole in one as you go through the maze.

WORD JIGSAW

Fit the pieces into the frame to form common words reading across and down. There's no need to rotate the pieces; they'll fit as shown, with each piece used once.

J A		D E
E E		R Y
M L	X	O
I L	E	B

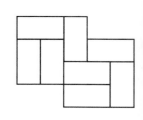

Answers on page 186.

MASTERMIND

The goal of this puzzle is to replace the question marks with a correct sequence of numbers. The numbers you need for the answer are contained in the rows above the question marks. Follow these 2 guides: A black dot indicates that a number needed for the solution is in that row and in the correct position; a white dot means that a number needed for the solution is in that row but in the wrong position. Numbers do not appear more than once in the solution, and the solution never begins with 0.

```
6 3 2 ○ ○
2 4 8 ○
5 6 0 ○
7 9 1 ●
─────────
? ? ?
```

CURVE FILL

Fill in each heavy-outlined set of cells with the same number (0, 2, or 5) so that the sums given for each curved row and column and the 2 sections extending from the center oval are true. For further insight, see the example puzzle at right.

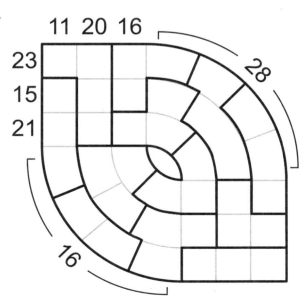

Answers on page 186.

GLOBE QUEST

Fly from Miami to Seattle, visiting each city once. See if you can find the cheapest route for your trip. Less than $410 would make you a Super Vacationer; less than $375, a Passport Pioneer; less than $354, a Seasoned Traveler. If you can make the trip for $335, then you're a Globe Quester!

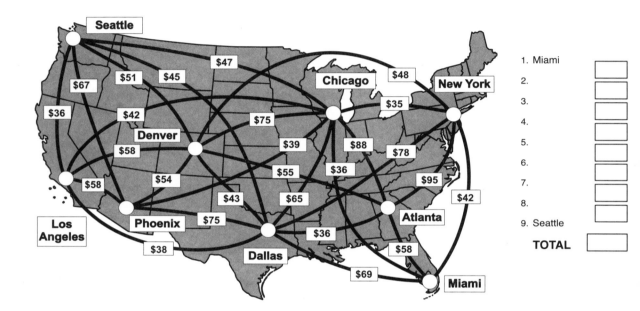

1. Miami

2.

3.

4.

5.

6.

7.

8.

9. Seattle

TOTAL

TRIVIA ON THE BRAIN
Between 15 percent and 20 percent of the body's oxygen is used by the brain.

Answer on page 186.

FIFTEEN UP

Divide the grid into 15 regions. The sum of each region must be 15. Numbers are used only once.

8	5	1	3	7	6	2
7	7	2	8	4	2	11
8	6	2	6	1	1	4
7	3	6	3	2	1	7
6	9	3	2	3	10	2
2	8	7	2	2	5	3
5	5	5	1	5	8	2

SUM FUN

In this grid, there are 29 instances where the sum of 38 can be obtained by adding numbers in a vertical, horizontal, or diagonal direction. Find and circle them all.

```
2 2 8 4 3 4 2 7 8 7 7 2
7 5 7 5 9 8 6 3 6 9 1 2
5 2 9 5 9 8 4 3 1 6 8 8
2 6 2 9 8 9 1 5 5 3 4 4
8 5 8 3 3 2 8 3 7 2 9 3
7 8 5 8 5 2 8 7 1 4 7 4
9 8 7 9 7 1 7 4 6 7 8 2
4 6 3 6 7 3 7 7 7 5 2 7
8 2 8 1 1 6 8 1 6 3 5 8
1 2 8 6 9 7 3 4 7 6 7 7
7 9 6 3 2 4 7 5 3 6 2 7
2 5 7 6 8 9 1 4 7 1 3 2
```

Answers on page 186.

ANIMAL RHYME

Find 8 pairs of words, each containing an animal, that rhyme.

Answers on page 187.

ELEVATOR WORDS

Like an elevator, words move up and down the "floors" of this puzzle. Starting with the first answer, the second word from each answer carries down to become the first part of the following answer. With the clues given, complete the puzzle.

1. Squawk _____   1. Intercom speaker

2. _____ _____   2. Slow-moving pet

3. _____   3. Type of sweater

4. _____ _____   4. Piece of equipment for an ice hockey player

5. _____ _____   5. Highway protection

6. _____ _____   6. Boundary made of split logs

7. _____ sitter   7. One who is undecided

X AND Y

If X and Y represent 2 different numbers from the list below, how many different values are possible for X times Y?

0, 1, 3, 5, 7

Answers on page 187.

KLUMP

Shade in some of the numbers so the remaining connected sets of numbers match the following sums:

2, 5, 8, 10, 17, 18

A solitary number (not connected to any other) can represent one or more of these sums.

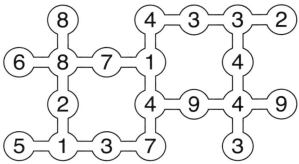

LOGINUMBER

Determine the values of the letters below using 2 rules: Each letter is no greater than the number of letters in the puzzle; none of the letters are equal to each other.

Use the grid to help keep track of possible solutions.

B + D = A

D + E = B

C + B + E = 10

	1	2	3	4	5
A					
B					
C					
D					
E					

Answers on page 187.

STAR POWER

Fill in each of the empty squares in the grid so that each star is surrounded by the numbers 1 through 8 with no repeats.

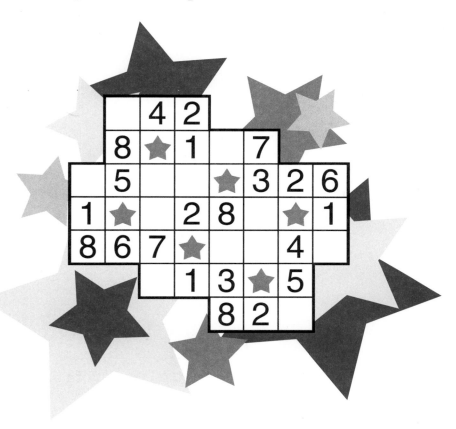

TRIVIA ON THE BRAIN
So much for rest! Most people have about 5 dreams during 8 hours of sleep. That adds up quickly—to about 1,825 dreams per year!

Answer on page 187.

ALIEN MUTATIONS

Shown are 12 mutation chambers surrounded by alien figures. Each of the 4 aliens on the left passed through the 3 chambers to their right and transformed into the figure on the other side (e.g. the alien on the left of A passed through chambers A, B, and C and mutated into the alien to the right of C). The same is true for the aliens above the chambers: Each passed through the 4 chambers directly below them and came out mutated on the other side.

Each chamber affects one—and only one—alteration (changes in head or body shape, changes in posture, addition/removal of appendages). Note: Some chambers in the same row or column will undo what a previous chamber has done.

What mutation is each chamber responsible for?

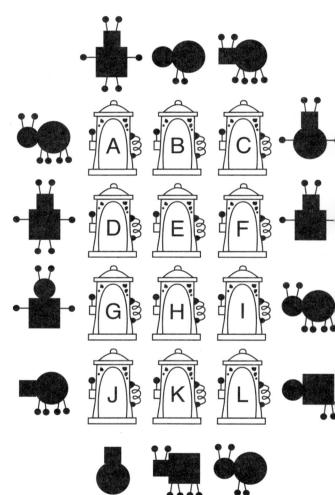

Answers on page 187.

GRID FILL

To complete this puzzle, place the given letters and words into the shapes in this grid. Words and letters will run across, down, and wrap around each shape. When the grid is filled, each row will contain one of the following words: bombs, camel, caved, early, files, resin.

1. Y

2. ERE

3. CAME, CAVE, FILM, LESS

4. BLIND, BOARS

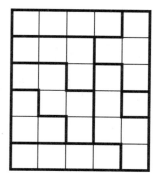

VEX-A-GON

Place the numbers 1 through 6 into the triangles of each hexagon. The numbers may be in any order, but they do not repeat within each hexagon shape.

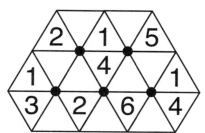

Answers on page 187.

CALCU-DOKU

Use arithmetic and deductive logic to complete the grid so that each row and column contains the numbers 1 through 5 in some order. Numbers in each outlined set of squares combine to produce the number in the top corner using the mathematical sign indicated.

24×		4+		6+
14+		2/	2/	
				6×
2-		1-		
1	6×		20×	

CROSS SUMS

Use the numbers below to fill in the grid. Each cell at the top of the 3 adjacent cells is the sum of numbers below it. So, as seen in the example, A=B+C+D. Here's the numbers needed to fill in the bottom 2 rows:

1 2 3 4 5 6 7 8 9 11 12 15 18

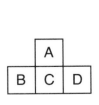

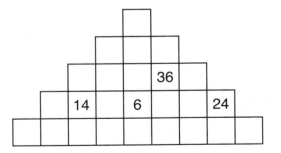

Answers on page 187.

INDOOR GAMES

Every word listed is contained within the group of letters. Words can be found in a straight line horizontally, vertically, or diagonally. They may be read either backward or forward. Leftover letters spell out a saying on the great indoors.

ACROSTICS

BACCARAT

BILLIARDS

BINGO

BOWLING

BRIDGE

CANASTA

CHARADES

CHESS

CROSSWORDS

DOMINOES

GO FISH

HEARTS

OLD MAID

PARCHEESI

PING-PONG

PINOCHLE

POKER

POOL

SCRABBLE

SNOOKER

SOLITAIRE

TABLE TENNIS

TIC-TAC-TOE

TIDDLYWINKS

VIDEO GAMES

WHIST

```
D I E R I A T I L O S L I K E
O W I N A C R O S T I C S T S
M E V I D E O G A M E S R S B
I E C A K P W S U S O E E K I
N C G O F I S H T C T H A N T
O A O C N S T E I R C A Y I A
E N O H G I N D L S A O O W R
S A L A N R S W P H T E I Y A
C S D R O W S S O R C T H L C
R T M A P H O O K U I O T D C
A A A D G F G E E E T L N D A
B I I E N N S D R A I L L I B
B N D S I N N E T E L B A T P
L G G B P A R C H E E S I U I
E G D I R B O W L I N G L T Y
```

Leftover letters: _____

Answers on page 187.

147

SPY FLY

As an international spy, your mission is to travel from your headquarters at Seth Castle to your safe house at Faro. To disguise your trail, you must stop once—and only once—at each airport. See if you can find the cheapest route for your trip. Less than $320 would make you a Steady Sleuth; less than $310, a Cool Operator; less than $300, a Crafty Agent. If you can make it on $260, then you're a Super Spy!

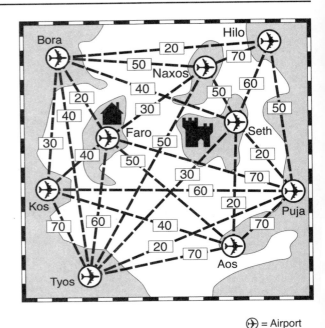

= Airport
= Start
= Finish

FILLOMINO

Fill in the grid with the numbers 1 through 4. Each number will be connected—horizontally or vertically—to a block of numbers all containing the same amount. So a cell with the number 2 in it will be connected to another cell with the number 2; a cell with the number 3 will be connected to two more cells with the number 3.

4	3	1	
3		3	
1	3	4	

Answers on page 188.

CODEWORD

The letters of the alphabet are hidden in code: They are represented by a random number from 1 through 26. With the letters already given, complete the crossword puzzle with English words and break the code.

1	18	14	17	⬛	19	15	25	11	5	10	5	11
5	⬛	18	⬛	4	⬛	24	⬛	9	⬛	5	⬛	5
16	9	13	5	10	4	12	⬛	1	21	5	8	3
3	⬛	5	⬛	8	⬛	26	⬛	21	⬛	25	⬛	5
9	13	1	5	25	⬛	5	23	5	14	4	15	10
2	⬛	⬛	⬛	1	⬛	25	⬛	8	⬛	10	⬛	5
20	8	18	25	14	21	⬛	14	10	8	12	15	25
15	⬛	4	⬛	5	⬛	8	⬛	4	⬛	⬛	⬛	4
10	5	9	26	25	5	11	⬛	5	25	25	18	9
4	⬛	16	⬛	11	⬛	23	⬛	25	⬛	15	⬛	8
8	16	9	6	5	⬛	18	25	5	7	18	8	16
25	⬛	22	⬛	25	⬛	10	⬛	11	⬛	25	⬛	16
4	19	5	25	4	9	5	1	⬛	5	1	20	12

A B C D E F G H I J K L M N O P Q R S T U V W X Y Z

1	2	3	4	5	6	7	8	9	10	11	12	13
										D		

14	15	16	17	18	19	20	21	22	23	24	25	26
				U							N	G

Answer on page 188.

SPLIT DECISIONS

Fill in each set of empty cells with letters that will create English words reading both across and down. Letters may repeat within a single set. We've completed one set to get you started.

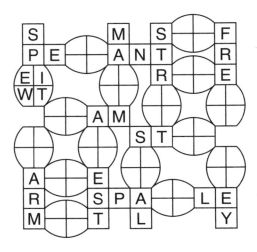

WORD LADDER

Use the clues to change just one letter on each line to go from the top word to the bottom word. Do not change the order of the letters. You must have a common English word at each step.

BIGOT

_____ to sire

_____ the past tense of the above

_____ started

_____ no animal product eaten

VEGAS

Answers on page 188.

NUMBER CROSSWORD

Fill in this crossword with numbers instead of letters. Use the clues to determine which number from 1 through 9 belongs in each square. No zeros are used.

ACROSS

1. Consecutive digits, increasing
4. The sum of its digits is 13
5. A perfect square
6. A palindrome

DOWN

1. Its last 3 digits are the same
2. Its middle 2 digits are the same
3. Square root of 1-Down
5. Square root of 2-Down

BATTLE BOATS

Place each ship in the fleet located at right within the grid. Ships may be placed horizontally or vertically, but they don't touch each other, not even diagonally. Numbers reveal the ship segments located in that row or column.

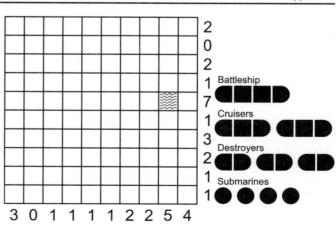

Answers on page 188.

TANGLEWORDS

Think of this puzzle like a word search, only in reverse. Rather than finding the words in the grid, your job is to fill them in. Words begin only from the letters given in the shaded boxes and they appear in a straight line diagonally, horizontally, or vertically. They may appear backward or forward. When complete, every word will have been used, and the grid will have no empty squares.

ABILITY

ABLER

ADORER

AERIAL

AIDES

AKIMBO

ALIASES

AMOEBA

ANGER

ANTEDATE

APLOMB

ASCOT

ASSAULT

ASTERISK

AUGUST

AWAITS

EARLY

EIDER

ELEGANT

ELLEN

ELVES

EMBARGO

EMBRYO

ENTRY

EXALTED

EXIT

EXPEDITE

IGNITE

INDEXES

INSANE

ODDS

ONEROUS

OPERA

OVER

UNCLOG

UNEQUAL

UNIFIES

UNSKILLED

UNTREATED

USAGES

USUAL

U-TURN

YEARS

YEOMEN

Answers on page 188.

CHAIN SUDOKU

Use deductive logic to complete the grid so that each row, each column, and each connected set of circles contains the numbers 1 through 5 in some order. The solution is unique.

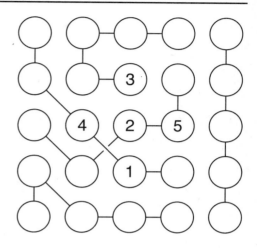

1-2-3

Place the numbers 1, 2, or 3 in the empty circles. The challenge is to have only these 3 numbers in each connected row and column—no number should repeat. Any combination is allowed.

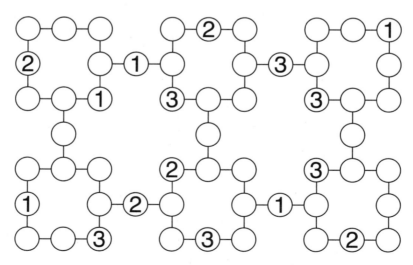

Answers on page 188.

ACROSTIC

Solve the clues below, and then place the letters in their corresponding spots in the grid to reveal a quote from Samuel Johnson. The letter in the upper-right corner of each grid square refers to the clue the letter comes from. A black square indicates the end of a word.

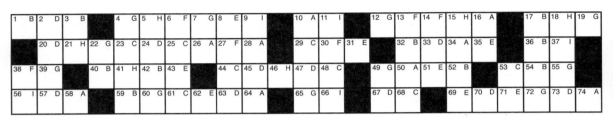

1 B	2 D	3 B		4 G	5 H	6 F	7 G	8 E	9 I		10 A	11 I		12 G	13 F	14 F	15 H	16 A		17 B	18 H	19 G
	20 D	21 H	22 G	23 C	24 D	25 C	26 A	27 F	28 A		29 C	30 F	31 E		32 B	33 D	34 A	35 E		36 B	37 I
38 F	39 G		40 B	41 H	42 B	43 E		44 C	45 D	46 H	47 D	48 C		49 G	50 A	51 E	52 B		53 C	54 B	55 G
56 I	57 D	58 A		59 B	60 G	61 C	62 E	63 D	64 A		65 G	66 I		67 D	68 C		69 E	70 D	71 E	72 G	73 D	74 A

A. Literary collection

____ ____ ____ ____ ____ ____ ____ ____ ____
34 74 16 50 10 26 58 64 28

B. Pest control device: 2 wds.

____ ____ ____ ____ ____ ____ ____ ____ ____ ____
40 42 52 59 32 17 1 36 3 54

C. Nobel _____

____ ____ ____ ____ ____ ____ ____ ____
48 25 44 61 23 53 29 68

D. Popular pattern in fabrics

____ ____ ____ ____ ____ ____ ____ ____ ____ ____ ____
2 33 70 24 47 63 20 67 57 45 73

E. Portable computer

____ ____ ____ ____ ____ ____ ____ ____
8 62 43 51 69 71 31 35

F. Rocky's surname

____ ____ ____ ____ ____ ____
14 6 27 38 30 13

G. Feature in a small apartment, perhaps

____ ____ ____ ____ ____ ____ ____ ____ ____ ____ ____
72 7 60 4 12 19 22 39 65 49 55

H. _____-or situation

____ ____ ____ ____ ____ ____
41 15 46 5 21 18

I. Pays for, as in a bill

____ ____ ____ ____ ____
11 37 66 56 9

Answers on page 189.

154

KAKURO

Place a number from 1 through 9 in each empty cell so that the sum of each vertical or horizontal run (rows and columns extending from already numbered cells) equals the number at the top or on the left of that run. Numbers may not be repeated in any run, and runs end at dark-colored squares.

ELEVATOR WORDS

Like an elevator, words move up and down the "floors" of this puzzle. Starting with the first answer, the second word from each answer carries down to become the first word of the following answer. With the clues given, complete the puzzle.

1. Weather _____   1. Form of forecast

2. _____ _____   2. E-mail/news client

3. _____ _____   3. It's faster than first class

4. _____ _____   4. Almost daily delivery spot

5. _____ _____   5. Competitive hobby

6. _____ _____   6. Type of track

7. _____ breaker   7. Trip switching device

Answers on page 189.

WATER TANKS

Each cubic tank holds 6 gallons of water. Fill in some of the tanks with water to satisfy the volume given in the rows and columns. Equilibrium must be met within each outlined set of tanks. Note that some tanks in rows or columns without specified amounts may be filled to meet this need.

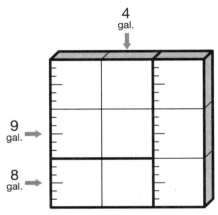

SQUARO

Shade in circles around each square as indicated by the numbers. For example, a square with a number 3 in it will have 3 of the 4 connected circles shaded in.

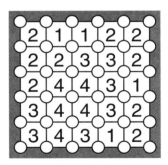

Answers on page 189.

EVENS/ODDS

Arrange the numbers 2, 4, and 6 horizontally and vertically in groups of three. Similarly, arrange the numbers 1, 3, and 5 into groups of three. Combinations connect with one another on shared numbers (a vertical 135 can connect with a horizontal 513) and the even and odd numbers will intertwine.

	5		4	
1		2		
	4		6	
2		3		4
6		5	2	
	4		1	

HITORI

The object of this puzzle is to have a number appear only once in each row and column. By shading a number cell, you are effectively removing that number from its row and column. There's a catch though: Shaded number cells are never adjacent to one another in a row or column.

7	5	9	4	4	3	2	1	8
9	5	7	3	8	6	1	2	1
3	5	8	5	2	7	6	5	1
2	2	2	1	7	9	9	3	6
4	6	5	3	3	8	7	1	9
8	9	1	7	6	1	2	6	5
2	3	1	6	5	8	4	4	7
1	7	7	5	8	3	6	8	2
2	8	4	8	6	5	5	9	2

Answers on page 189.

Below is a chain of continuous words. Start at clue number 1 and write the answers to the clues in the order they are given. Every answer overlaps the next one by one letter or more. If done correctly, the shaded rows will spell out 5 official positions.

1. Cut the grass

2. Reason

3. Follow, result

4. Lured

5. Sag

6. North or South…

7. Of horses

8. Weird

9. Birds of prey

10. Remove completely

11. Mars is one

12. Excursions

13. Odd

14. Thesis paper

15. Pull, jerk

16. Japanese attire

17. Large sea

18. A small European country

19. Representatives

20. Type, kind

21. Desire to drink

22. Homage

23. Narrate

24. Idle

25. Sana is its capital

26. Candidate

27. Boredom

Answers on page 189.

BATTLE BOATS

Place each ship in the fleet located at right within the grid. Ships may be placed horizontally or vertically, but they don't touch each other, not even diagonally. Numbers reveal the ship segments located in that row or column. Some segments have been added to get you started.

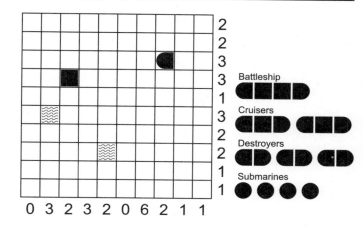

2
2
3
3
1

Battleship

3

Cruisers

2

Destroyers

2

Submarines

1

1

0 3 2 3 2 0 6 2 1 1

HOW'S YOUR RECALL? (PART I)

Study these items for one minute, then turn the page for a memory challenge.

Opera Glasses

Basketball Hoop

Toy Car

Treasure Chest

Key Chain

Taj Mahal

Camp Tent

Gumball Machine

Picture Frame

Answer on page 189.

HOW'S YOUR RECALL? (PART II)

Do not read this until you have read the previous page!

Check off the 2-word captions you remember from the previous page:

___ MOUNT FUJI

___ LOTTERY MACHINE

___ KEY CHAIN

___ VERDI'S "AIDA"

___ BASKETBALL COURT

___ HORSE OPERA

___ PICTURE FRAME

___ CAMP TENT

___ TAPE MEASURE

___ PINKING SHEARS

___ HULA HOOP

___ OPERA GLASSES

___ FISHING ROD

___ TREASURE CHEST

___ EIFFEL TOWER

L'ADDER

Starting at the bottom rung, use the numbers 1 through 9 to add up to the top number. Numbers can only be used once. The precise sums must be met along the way.

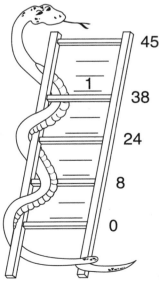

45

1   38

24

8

0

Answers on pages 189–190.

ABCD

Every cell in this grid contains 1 of 4 letters: A, B, C, or D. No letter can be horizontally or vertically adjacent to itself. The tables above and to the left of the grid indicate how many times each letter appears in that column or row. Can you complete the grid?

A	2	2	1	2	1	2	1	1	2
B	2	1	0	1	1	2	1	2	0
C	1	2	2	2	1	1	2	0	1
D	1	1	3	1	3	1	2	3	3

A	B	C	D									
1	3	2	3									
4	2	1	2									
2	2	0	5			B						
3	1	3	2									
2	2	1	4			A						
2	0	5	2									

TRIVIA ON THE BRAIN

Sudoku can loosely be traced back to a game called Latin Squares, which was developed in the 18th century by Swiss mathematician Leonhard Euler.

Answer on page 190.

MEND THE BRIDGES

Rain has swept through the entire county, flooding all the bridges (indicated by circles). Your job is to travel to each location—**A** through **I,** in any order—by restoring only 2 of the bridges.

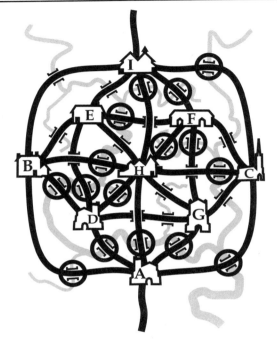

CRYPTO-LOGIC

Each of the numbers in the sequence below represents a letter. Use the mathematical clues to determine which number stands for which letter and reveal the encrypted word.

4 9 1 4 3 8 5

Clues:

I squared = E

(E + 1) ÷ U = G

2A = U

A = 1

G = R + A

R repeats

N = 2R

Answers on page 190.

LOGINUMBER

Determine the values of the letters below using 2 rules: Each letter is no greater than the number of letters in the puzzle; none of the letters are equal to each other.

Use the grid to help keep track of possible solutions.

C + D = A

D + A = B

	1	2	3	4
A				
B				
C				
D				

OPPOSITES

Use the letters below to fill in the boxes and reveal the 2 related words. Connected boxes share the same letter.

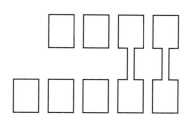

ESHOGTU

Answers on page 190.

This puzzle works exactly like a crossword, except instead of placing one letter in each box, you place 2. Words are written across in each box. As a bonus, unscramble the 10 letters found in the shaded boxes to answer the definition below.

ACROSS
1. Echo, grumble
5. Reversal, upset
6. Bring to a close
8. Least dirty
10. Financial
11. Cause to float

DOWN
2. Isolation
3. All people
4. Rare
7. Formal noon meal
8. Collarbone
9. Like a star

Unplanned: _____

Answers on page 190.

Place an X or an O inside each empty cell of the grid so that there appears no row, column, or diagonal with 4 consecutive cells with the same letter.

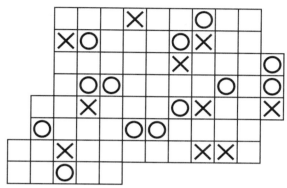

ACROSS THE BOARD

Fill in the grid with a path of consecutive numbers starting at 1 and ending at 81. Numbers may connect vertically, horizontally, or diagonally.

				10		27		
5	14	12	11		32		30	
					34	35		38
	17							
18						48		51
20	21			(1)	44	46		
60	59					54		71
		64				69		
(81)	80	65			76			

Answers on page 190.

ANSWERS

Chain Grid Fill (page 6)

A	H	P	R	D

R	M	N	A	S	O	S	O	L	O	P
A	E	U	R	L	R	I	C	E	W	A
D	R	D	D	I	T	L	K	M	N	R
I	I	W	G	L	V	W	O	T	R	
U	C	T	A	H	A	E	E	N	O	O
S	A	Y	R	T	N	R	L	S	W	T
		N		E		D		L		

Opposites (page 6)

| S | A | D |

| H | A | P | P | Y |

Sum Fun (page 7)

2	8	1	6	6	5	1	6
2	8	5	3	2	6	9	9
3	5	3	6	5	1	5	5
4	4	9	3	1	2	5
8	1	7	6	4	1	5	6
2	1	3	7	9	2	6	8
7	4	6	2	3	5	1	4
8	2	7	3	3	9	3	7

Across the Board (page 7)

58	57	55	54	53	35	34	32
59	56	61	62	36	52	31	33
41	60	43	37	63	51	28	30
40	42	38	44	50	64	27	29
10	39	12	46	45	49	24	26
9	11	5	13	47	48	25	23
8	2	6	4	14	17	19	22
1	7	3	15	16	18	20	21

Starstruck (page 8)

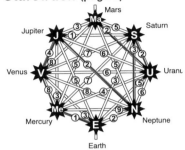

Sequence of letters:

| E | Me | V | J | N | S | U | Ma |

Days by spacecraft:

| 1 | 8 | 4 | 2 | 3 | 2 | 2 | = 22 |

Water Tanks (page 8)

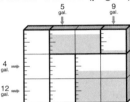

Word Sums (page 9)

```
    3 2 1
    3 2 1
    3 2 1
+   3 2 1
---------
  1 2 8 4
```

Frame Games™ (page 9)

Growing pains

Spy Fly (page 10)

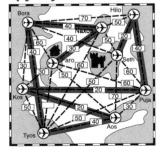

Klump (page 10)

Word Spiral (page 11)

W	I	N	D	O	W	N	E	R
N	T	R	A	P	P	O	R	S
E	E	R	E	W	I	T	T	H
M	H	T	A	M	E	H	E	I
I	W	S	E		N	A	N	P
T	Y	Y	L	B	A	L	T	W
N	R	R	T	S	E	V	O	R
E	E	V	E	E	L	S	U	E
S	S	E	L	E	G	A	K	C

3-D Word Search (page 12)

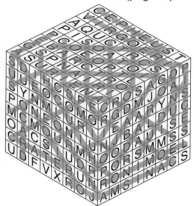

Runaway Train (page 13)

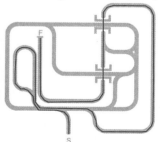

Magic Square (page 13)

2	9	11	16
15	12	6	5
8	3	17	10
13	14	4	7

Arrow Word (page 14)

SquarO (page 15)

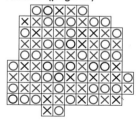

Futoshiki (page 15)

2	6	1	3	4	5
3	2	5	4	1	6
4	3	6	1	5	2
5	1	3	2	6	4
1	5	4	6	2	3
6	4	2	5	3	1

XOXO (page 16)

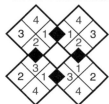

Black Diamonds (page 16)

Number Cross (page 17)

1	8	1	6	5	2	■	3	2	2	3	4	4
7	■	1	■	1	3	1	9	8	■	1	■	8
2	1	3	0	2	2	■	2	8	7	1	8	3
4	■	7	■	2	7	1	0	8	■	4	■	0
1	3	3	2	■	1	1	5	■	3	0	4	0
3	0	5	0	4	■	9	■	1	0	3	3	0
■	7	■	2	4	8	■	1	0	8	■	9	■
1	1	5	3	7	■	3	■	4	4	1	4	3
5	8	8	8	■	2	2	4	■	3	4	0	1
1	■	8	■	2	9	3	2	5	■	5	■	2
4	0	1	7	6	7	■	1	3	5	1	9	2
2	■	6	■	5	2	8	8	2	■	4	■	3
5	0	2	6	5	2	■	4	8	6	3	1	5

Acrostic (page 18)

"My feeling is that there is nothing in life but refraining from hurting others, and comforting those that are sad."

A. imitator; B. affront; C. infirmities; D. butterfly; E. Nightingale; F. orchestrated; G. Rhinestone; H. hangman; I. horseshoed; J. Gunfight

Fillomino (page 19)

2	2	1	3	3	1	4	4	4
4	4	4	3	2	3	1	4	
2	8	8	8	1	2	3	3	1
2	8	7	8	3	3	4	4	3
8	8	7	7	3	1	3	4	3
8	7	7	4	4	4	3	4	3
7	7	3	2	1	4	3	9	9
4	4	3	2	3	9	9	9	9
4	4	3	1	3	3	9	9	9

Neighborhood (page 19)

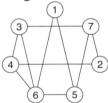

Mechanic Shop (page 20)

1. window in door now round; 2. rag missing from trash can; 3. hubcap different; 4. wrench got smaller; 5. shadow on hood elongated; 6. cap turned around; 7. wrench head added; 8. cord got shorter; 9. hanging parts missing; 10. coffee mug vanished; 11. workstation drawer altered; 12. wires missing; 13. screwdriver rolled away; 14. tread pattern different; 15. cord from overhead light missing

LogiNumber (page 21)

A = 7, B = 2, C = 1, D = 5, E = 6, F = 3, G = 4

Minesweeper (page 21)

✹	2				2	✹
✹		1		1	✹	
✹		✹		1		2	✹
	2		1				2
	1		1			1	✹
		✹					
	1		2	1		1	
			1	✹	2	✹	

Guess the Holiday (pages 22–23)

H	A	R	D	■	E	D	I	T	■	A	T	B	A	T
E	R	I	E	■	R	O	L	E	■	D	U	A	N	E
R	E	D	W	H	I	T	E	A	N	D	B	L	U	E
O	N	E	■	O	K	E	D	■	A	W	A	I	T	S
N	A	R	C	S	■	■	E	T	N	A	■			
■	■	L	E	A	D	■	O	U	T	F	L	O	W	
A	S	T	A	■	H	A	I	R	■	E	L	O	P	E
S	T	A	R	S	A	N	D	S	T	R	I	P	E	S
N	O	S	E	E	■	G	O	O	D	■	M	E	L	T
O	A	K	T	R	E	E	■	S	S	N	S	■		
■	■		I	N	R	E	■	■	E	Y	E	O	N	
A	P	E	M	A	N	■	A	L	A	N	■	M	S	G
G	O	D	B	L	E	S	S	A	M	E	R	I	C	A
R	O	G	A	N	■	H	E	R	E	■	A	L	A	I
A	R	E	S	O	■	E	L	A	N	■	T	Y	R	O

Evens/Odds (page 24)

	2	■	2	4	6
5	4	5	1	3	2
1	6	3	2	6	4
3	5	1	4	■	
■	■		6	2	4

Fifteen Up (page 24)

3	6	5	9	1	5	8
2	5	2	4	4	2	1
5	1	8	3	2	5	9
8	5	2	10	5	3	7
5	3	5	4	1	5	6
1	5	5	2	1	4	10
4	6	9	4	10	1	4

Pythagorize It! (page 25)

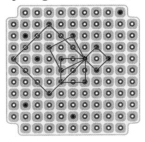

Elevator Words (page 26)

1. DECAF coffee; 2. coffee break; 3. break ground; 4. ground round; 5. round robin; 6. Robin Hood; 7. hood ORNAMENT

Calcu-doku (page 26)

4	2	1	3	6	5
1	4	5	6	2	3
3	6	2	4	5	1
6	1	4	5	3	2
2	5	3	1	4	6
5	3	6	2	1	4

Split Decisions (page 27)

Answers may vary.

Number Crossword (page 27)

		4	7	3
	7	6	5	4
6	2	1	6	
9	9	9		

Continuous (page 28)

Quipu (page 29)

A

Cross Sums (page 29)

			411					
		166	137	108				
	65	56	45	36	27			
24	23	18	15	12	9	6		
7	9	8	6	4	5	3	1	2

Word Jigsaw (page 30)

HUB
ARRAY
SNIDE
MOW

Marbles (page 30)

Sudoku (page 31)

6	3	9	7	1	5	2	8	4
4	5	2	8	6	3	9	1	7
1	8	7	2	4	9	3	6	5
9	1	8	4	5	6	7	2	3
3	7	4	9	2	8	6	5	1
5	2	6	3	7	1	8	4	9
8	4	5	6	3	7	1	9	2
7	6	1	5	9	2	4	3	8
2	9	3	1	8	4	5	7	6

Vex-a-Gon (page 31)

Curve Fill (page 32)

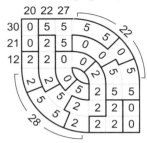

Addagram (page 32)

The missing letter is **Z**.

Tweezers, bronze, gazelle, citizen

Honeycomb (page 33)

Fitting Words (page 34)

T	A	F	F	Y
E	X	I	L	E
A	L	L	O	W
K	E	E	P	S

Hitori (page 34)

2	5	9	5	6	1	3	1	8
8	7	2	2	9	9	6	4	1
7	8	5	3	2	1	9	3	4
1	4	3	1	2	6	5	5	2
9	4	2	4	8	1	5	3	6
6	9	3	4	1	7	5	2	6
5	6	7	4	4	5	1	8	3
3	1	6	9	8	7	8	9	
4	3	3	7	9	2	9	6	8

Word-a-Maze: A Zoo in a Box (page 35)

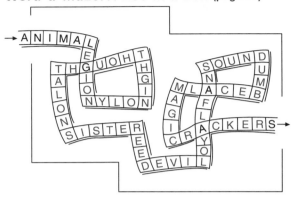

Mend the Bridges (page 36)

Answers may vary.

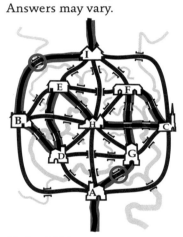

Futoshiki (page 36)

3	4	6	1	2	5
2	1	4	5	6	3
4	3	1	2	5	6
1	2	5	6	3	4
6	5	2	3	4	1
5	6	3	4	1	2

Kakuro (page 37)

			3	1		
		2	1	4		
	9	1		7	9	8
	8	7	9		1	3
		1	2	3		
		7	9			

SquarO (page 37)

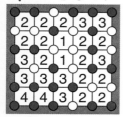

Chain Sudoku (page 38)

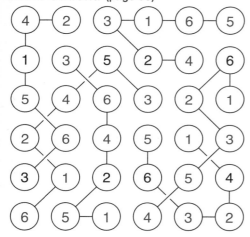

Perfect Score (page 38)

30+30+40=100

Grammy Hall of Fame Awards (page 39)

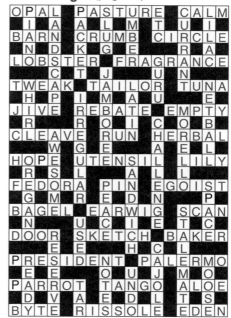

The leftover letters spell: "This is a partial list of dozens of performers honored by the award."

Stretch! (pages 40–41)

A	G	E	D	■	O	P	T	■	W	H	O	S

AGED ■ OPT ■ WHOS
TAXI ■ LEO ■ OURS
AGAS ■ ANNARBOR
BACKOFNECK ■ ■
■ TSO ■ HELGA
ESC ■ HAMSTRING
MOON ■ TEA ■ SMUT
UPPERARMS ■ ESS
SAYSO ■ ■ CAW ■
■ QUADRICEPS
BEAUTIES ■ ODIE
AMBI ■ DEV ■ IGET
ROCK ■ EMP ■ NESS

Letter Logic (page 42)

OPAL ■ PASTURE ■ CALM
I ■ A ■ A ■ L ■ T ■ U ■ I
BARN ■ CRUMB ■ CIRCLE
N ■ D ■ K ■ G ■ E ■ R ■ A
LOBSTER ■ FRAGRANCE
C ■ T ■ J ■ U ■ N
TWEAK ■ TAILOR ■ TUNA
H ■ P ■ I ■ M ■ A ■ U ■ E
JIVE ■ REBATE ■ EMPTY
R ■ R ■ O ■ I ■ C ■ O ■ B
CLEAVE ■ RUN ■ HERBAL
W ■ G ■ E ■ A ■ E ■ L
HOPE ■ UTENSIL ■ LILY
R ■ S ■ L ■ A ■ L ■ L
FEDORA ■ PIN ■ EGOIST
G ■ M ■ R ■ E ■ D ■ N ■ P
BAGEL ■ EARWIG ■ SCAN
N ■ D ■ U ■ C ■ I ■ E ■ T ■ C
DOOR ■ SKETCH ■ BAKER
E ■ E ■ H ■ C ■ L
PRESIDENT ■ PALERMO
E ■ E ■ O ■ J ■ M ■ O
PARROT ■ TANGO ■ ALOE
D ■ V ■ A ■ E ■ D ■ L ■ T ■ S
BYTE ■ RISSOLE ■ EDEN

Word Columns (page 43)

Two farmers each claimed to own a certain cow. While one pulled on its head and the other pulled on its tail, the cow was milked by a lawyer.

Alien Mutations (page 44)

A. head square; B. add antennae; C. body circle; D. remove rear appendages; E. body square; F. to biped; G. to quadruped; H. add front appendages; I. remove antennae

Klump (page 45)

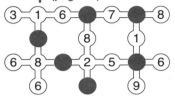

Hashi (page 45)

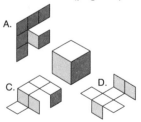

ABCD (page 46)

D	B	C	B	C	B
C	D	A	C	D	A
A	C	D	A	B	C
C	D	A	D	C	B
D	B	D	C	D	C
B	C	A	B	C	A

Cube Fold (page 47)

A.

C.   D.

Word Jigsaw (page 47)

G	A	P	
A	L	L	O	W
B	L	A	D	E
	N	E	T	

Knot Problem (page 48)

A and C contain a knot.

Vex-a-Gon (page 48)

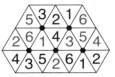

Red, White, and Blue (page 49)

B	R	B	W	W	R
R	W	W	B	R	B
B	W	R	B	R	W
R	B	W	R	W	B
W	B	R	W	B	R
W	R	B	R	B	W

Cross Scan (pages 50–51)

1. New; 2. York; 3. city; 4. mets; 5. park;
6. Grand; 7. upper; 8. river; 9. radio; 10. music;
11. opera; 12. museum; 13. Harlem; 14. Gotham;
15. Empire 16. tunnel; 17. giants; 18. Subway;
19. square; 20. island; 21. bridge; 22. Madison;
23. Chelsea; 24. village; 25. battery; 26. Central;
27. Yankees; 28. Yeshiva; 29. rangers;
30. Columbia; 31. Carnegie; 32. big apple;
33. Amsterdam; 34. "Manhattan";
35. Greenwich; 36. "Chinatown";
37. Washington

Leftover letters spell: The melting pot cooks up a rich, creative stew.

Theme: New York City

Slitherlink Path (page 52)

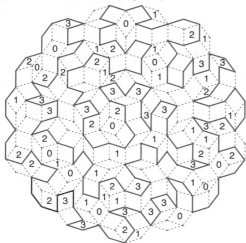

Fillomino (page 53)

4	7	7	8	7	3	3	3	7
4	4	7	8	7	7	7	7	7
1	4	7	8	8	8	8	6	6
4	7	7	8	8	6	6	6	4
4	7	2	2	1	8	8	6	4
4	4	3	3	3	7	8	4	4
1	7	7	7	7	7	8	3	3
8	8	8	8	4	7	8	8	3
8	8	8	8	4	4	4	8	8

Fifteen Up (page 53)

4	5	7	5	5	5	3	9
2	2	3	5	1	2	7	
2	5	4	9	8	2	6	
1	3	8	6	6	1	3	
1	6	6	12	3	1	10	
5	7	9	1	1	12	2	
1	2	3	4	11	1	3	

Star Power (page 54)

6	5	1	8	2			
8	★	7	★	5	8	2	5	7
3	2	4	3	6	★	1	★	4
7	★	1	★	7	4	3	6	8	2
6	5	8	2	5	8	★	7	★	4
	1	★	4	★	1	2	5	1	3
	6	3	7	3	6	★	8	★	7
					3	7	4	6	2

Mastermind (page 55)

23461

Times Square (page 55)

2	1	2	2
7	7	1	3
1	5	5	2
7	5	8	1

1-2-3 (page 56)

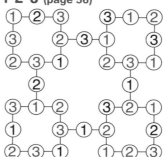

Crypto-Logic (page 56)

DONE

Add-a-Letter (page 57)

```
W B R O T H E R B O R D E R E
P O S S E S S F A K I R V O K
L G Z G S P A R K J S A R U O
U D N N M R J D O P E E U S O
N R J I P O P U L A R B C E R
G E E K R U S I N G L I N G C
E T N L R T C E R E L A T E M
X A O A G E S E V A R C N A N
U E I W K N A L H L T K E G O
H W T Y C T A D P C O R I X R
S S C R E N O D N E T S T D E
U P A R T L Y A O S E A A R H
L M R L S C A P E D M W P O G
P O F A C T O R T R E A S O N
R E V E A L C O A S T E R P J
```

On Your Mark, Get Set... (page 58)

1. Hair color is different; 2. wristband is missing; 3. railing post added; 4. stripe on shorts erased; 5. socks have fewer stripes; 6. facial hair added; 7. track has extra lane; 8. runner's number added a 1; 9. "team" spelled "teem"; 10. shoes changed color

Across the Board (page 59)

43	44	30	29	28	25	26
37	42	45	31	32	27	24
38	36	41	46	33	23	21
39	40	35	34	47	22	20
11	10	9	48	7	19	5
12	15	(49)	8	18	6	4
13	14	16	17	(1)	2	3

Grid Fill (page 59)

S	P	A	I	N
A	R	S	O	N
V	E	S	T	S
I	G	L	O	O
S	T	R	I	P
A	M	P	L	E

Globe Quest (page 60)

1. Miami
2. Atlanta — 32
3. Denver — 69
4. New York — 77
5. Chicago — 26
6. Los Angeles — 40
7. Phoenix — 42
8. Dallas — 49
9. Seattle — 35

TOTAL — 370

Mend the Bridges (page 60)

Answers may vary.

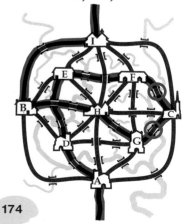

Battle Boats (page 61)

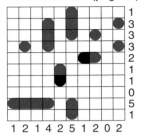

Vex-a-Gon (page 61)

Minesweeper (page 62)

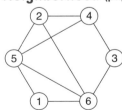

Addagram (page 62)

The missing letter is **U**.
Ritual, nucleus, lucrative, altruism

Neighborhood (page 63)

Logidoku (page 63)

6	3	4	1	8	5	7	2	9
5	8	7	9	2	4	3	1	6
2	1	9	3	6	7	8	5	4
3	4	8	5	9	2	1	6	7
1	2	6	8	7	3	9	4	5
9	7	5	6	4	1	2	8	3
8	9	3	2	5	6	4	7	1
7	5	2	4	1	9	6	3	8
4	6	1	7	3	8	5	9	2

XOXO (page 64)

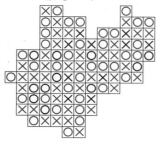

Hashi (page 64)

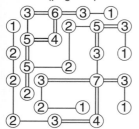

Starstruck (page 65)

Sequence of letters:

E	N	Me	U	S	J	V	Ma

Days by spacecraft:

1	6	8	2	2	1	1	= 21

SquarO (page 65)

Fitting Words (page 66)

S	A	M	B	A
O	B	O	E	S
F	L	A	S	K
T	E	N	T	S

Frame Games™ (page 66)

A word to the wise is sufficient.

Flowers (page 67)

1	2	3	4	5	6	7	8	9	10	11	12	13
O	R	C	H	I	D	J	Z	X	W	T	S	E

14	15	16	17	18	19	20	21	22	23	24	25	26
A	B	K	N	Q	U	Y	P	L	G	M	F	V

Water Tanks (page 68)

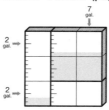

Minesweeper (page 68)

175

Codeword (page 69)

```
  S   Q   R     F   L   D
S P R U C E   A M A Z O N
  U   E   L   I   U   W
O D E S   A R R O G A N T
  T   X   S   H   T
J U P I T E R   T I B I A
  P   O   D   D   N   M
S H O N E   W E I G H E D
  E   N   T   C   S
C A V A L I E R   T E S T
  V   I   L   Y   O   K
J A R R E D   P I C N I C
  L   E   E   T   K   D
```

1	2	3	4	5	6	7	8	9	10	11	12	13
Y	K	J	F	I	B	A	G	H	L	V	C	P

14	15	16	17	18	19	20	21	22	23	24	25	26
M	E	O	Z	S	D	U	W	X	N	R	T	Q

Shrouded Summary (page 70)

During Dresden bombing, Second World War prisoner encounters aliens, inheriting time-jumping experience where his past, present, and future appear randomly. "Slaughterhouse-Five" by Kurt Vonnegut

Kakuro (page 71)

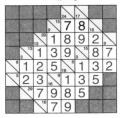

Word Ladder (page 71)

BRUSH, brash, crash, clash, class, crass, BRASS

Continuous (page 72)

Perfect Score (page 73)

22+30+48=100

Word Jigsaw (page 73)

```
O W L
A H E A D
K O A L A
  F E D
```

Open Up! (pages 74–75)

S	T	E	M	■	T	R	O	N	■	G	E	C	K	O
L	O	V	E	■	I	O	W	A	■	U	N	H	I	P
E	D	E	N	■	M	O	N	K	E	Y	D	I	E	U
D	A	N	U	B	E	■	S	E	C	■	E	L	L	S
S	Y	S	■	A	L	G	■	D	U	B	A	I	■	■
■	■	H	A	I	R	Y	■	■	O	R	D	E	R	■
E	S	M	E	■	M	E	A	G	E	R	■	O	C	A
O	P	E	N	M	I	C	K	E	Y	N	I	G	H	T
N	E	D	■	O	T	O	O	L	E	■	T	S	O	S
S	W	I	R	L	■	■	V	I	O	L	A	■	■	■
■	C	O	L	I	C	■	D	P	T	■	M	I	A	■
O	H	I	O	■	C	A	L	■	E	D	W	A	R	D
D	O	N	K	E	Y	J	U	A	N	■	A	X	E	D
E	M	A	I	L	■	U	R	G	E	■	W	I	N	E
S	E	L	E	S	■	N	E	A	R	■	A	M	E	R

Tanglewords (page 78)

K	C	A	B	A	C	A	P	S	I	Z	E	D
K	C	A	L	B	T	A	L	E	N	T	E	D
I	A	A	M	E	T	H	Y	S	T	S	N	N
S	S	O	R	T	A	B	L	A	A	A	I	O
S	C	B	E	T	L	L	B	E	R	A	L	I
E	E	R	R	I	K	O	R	L	T	G	P	S
R	N	E	M	N	A	C	E	P	A	I	I	I
S	D	P	A	G	T	K	A	U	N	R	C	V
T	I	U	C	R	I	C	D	B	I	Y	S	I
U	N	S	R	E	V	I	T	C	E	R	I	D
L	G	H	O	E	E	E	H	C	T	I	D	B
I	C	E	S	R	S	E	R	A	W	A	N	U
P	O	S	S	E	S	S	C	Y	T	H	E	S

Grid Fill (page 76)

T	O	M	A	T	O
S	T	R	E	A	M
S	A	V	E	R	S
T	H	O	R	N	Y
B	O	U	G	H	T
P	A	P	E	R	S
C	R	E	A	T	E

Black Diamonds (page 76)

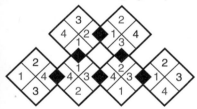

Futoshiki (page 77)

4	5	2	1	3	6
3	4	1	2	6 > 5	
6	2 < 5	3 < 4	1		
1	6	4	5	2	3
2 > 1	3	6 > 5 > 4			
5 > 3	6	4	1	2	

Calcu-doku (page 77)

4	5	1	2	3
2	3	5	1	4
3	2	4	5	1
5	1	3	4	2
1	4	2	3	5

L'adder (page 79)

Answers may vary.

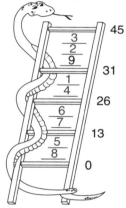

$$\frac{3}{2}{9} \quad 45$$
$$\frac{1}{4} \quad 31$$
$$26$$
$$\frac{6}{7} \quad 13$$
$$\frac{5}{8} \quad 0$$

Fillomino (page 79)

8	4	4	4	3	3	2	2
8	8	8	7	3	7	4	4
8	3	3	3	7	7	7	4
8	4	4	4	4	6	6	7	4
8	1	2	2	1	8	6	6	6
1	8	8	3	3	8	8	8	6
8	8	8	6	3	1	8	8	3
8	6	6	6	6	8	8	2	3
8	8	6	3	3	3	1	2	3

3-D Word Search (page 80)

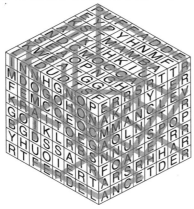

Across the Board (page 81)

3	4	5	6	36	37	38
29	2	(1)	7	35	39	40
28	30	32	34	8	41	42
27	31	33	9	10	11	43
26	24	23	22	14	44	12
25	18	21	15	45	13	48
19	20	17	16	46	47	(49)

Evens/Odds (page 81)

Digital Sudoku (page 82)

```
3 2 6 5 1 4
4 5 1 2 3 6
1 6 2 3 4 5
5 3 4 6 2 1
2 4 5 1 6 3
6 1 3 4 5 2
```

Addagram (page 82)
The missing letter is **C.**
Crimson, monarchy, chronicle, nuclear

Arrow Word (page 83)

	C	L		T		U		C
R	A	Z	E		O	P	E	N	E	R
	I	E	U	R	O		T		M	A
	R	R		S	P	R	I	G	S
L	O	S	S		O	S	I	E	R	S
	Y		P			D		O	Harp
H	A	R	S	H		M	E	D	A	L
C	U	P	O	L	A		A	N	Y
P	I	P	I	T		U	N	D	E	R
D		T	O	L	L		O	D	E

Minesweeper (page 84)

Split Decisions (page 84)
Answers may vary.

Hamster Treadmill (page 85)
Devices A and C are correct.

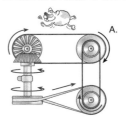
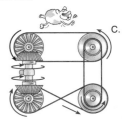

178

All in the Family (pages 86–87)

The leftover letters spell: Ken Griffey and Ken Griffey Jr. and Tim Raines and Tim Raines Jr. were the only father-son teammates in MLB.

Math Class (page 87)

35. Two negatives make a positive.

Lotus Maze (page 88)

Crack the Code (page 89)

☆ = 1   ♣ = 4   ♦ = 7   ☀ = 9

Perfect Score (page 89)

1+15+84=100

Odd-Even Logidoku (page 90)

7	5	4	3	8	9	2	6	1
1	6	3	2	7	4	9	5	8
9	2	8	1	6	5	3	4	7
2	8	7	5	1	6	4	9	3
3	1	9	8	4	2	5	7	6
5	4	6	7	9	3	8	1	2
6	3	2	9	5	7	1	8	4
4	9	1	6	3	8	7	2	5
8	7	5	4	2	1	6	3	9

Spell Math! (page 90)

Six + three = nine

What's On? (page 91)

1	2	3	4	5	6	7	8	9	10	11	12	13
T	V	N	A	M	E	S	G	X	Z	I	D	P
14	15	16	17	18	19	20	21	22	23	24	25	26
O	C	U	H	R	K	J	W	Y	L	F	B	Q

Missing Details (page 92)

Word Columns (page 93)

"The hottest place in Hell is reserved for those who remain neutral in times of great moral conflict."

Vex-a-Gon (page 93)

Doubled Up (page 94)

The 10-letter word is: Torrential

```
      A P P R A I S E
            E S         S P
  S C     S U P E R I O R
  A L B A C O R E       A D
  L I     I F   P A R T I C L E
  O N     F U   S T       C T
      T O R E A D O R     U R
            A L L O T T E D
```

LogiNumber (page 95)

$A = 5, B = 4, C = 7, D = 6, E = 2, F = 8, G = 3, H = 1$

Word Sums (page 95)

```
   2 4 1 8 3
   2 4 1 8 3
   2 4 1 8 3
 + 2 4 1 8 3
   9 6 7 3 2
```

Crack the Code (page 96)

▲ = 1   ◆ = 4   ✿ = 6   ❑ = 7

● = 8   ✳ = 9   ◯ = 10

Opposites (page 96)

```
W A X
W A N E
```

Battle Boats (page 97)

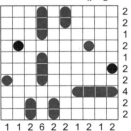

Black Diamonds (page 97)

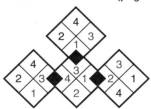

Kitchen Utensils (pages 98–99)

```
C R A V E   E S S   F L O
L E W I S   A H A   R I D
U B O L T   R A Y M O N D
B A L L O O N W H I S K
      A N I   L I N T
O B I   I N C   O I L S
P A N C A K E T U R N E R
T A C H   O W N   G E O
      L I S T   I S M
      L O C K I N G T O N G S
B I V O U A C   I R A N I
A T E   N R A   C O N A N
H E R   K A A   K N O T S
```

Pray, But Keep Your Eyes Open (page 99)

"When the missionaries came to Africa they had the Bible and we had the land. They said, 'Let us pray.' We closed our eyes. When we opened them we had the Bible and they had the land."

—Bishop Desmond Tutu

Number Search (page 100)

Get It Straight (page 101)

Addagram (page 101)

The missing letter is **C**.
Escargot, scalpel, crescendo, drastic

Evens/Odds (page 102)

	4	2	6
3	6	■	
1	2	4	6
5	3	1	2
	2	6	4

Klump (page 102)

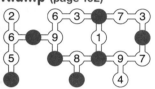

Fifteen Up (page 103)

10	2	3	7	3	2	8
2	2	8	6	5	3	2
1	9	2	11	3	1	7
2	6	4	4	2	10	3
7	6	1	3	2	1	5
6	5	3	12	3	5	10
1	5	2	7	1	7	5

Cross Sums (page 103)

			104			
		25	34	45		
	6	7	12	15	18	
3	1	2	4	6	5	7

Literary Search (page 104)

1. "The Catcher in the Rye"; 2. "Catch-22";
3. "One Flew Over the Cuckoo's Nest";
4. "The Fountainhead"; 5. "The Kite Runner";
6. "Harry Potter and the Goblet of Fire";
7. "Little Women"; 8. "The Bell Jar"

Sum Fun (page 105)

2	2	8	4	3	4	2	7	8	7
7	5	7	5	9	8	6	3	6	9
5	2	9	5	9	4	3	1	6	5
2	6	2	9	8	9	1	5	5	3
8	5	8	3	3	2	8	7	1	4
7	8	5	8	5	2	8	7	1	4
9	8	7	9	7	1	7	4	6	7
4	6	3	6	7	3	7	7	5	1
8	2	8	1	6	8	1	6	3	5
1	2	8	6	9	7	3	4	7	6

Minesweeper (page 105)

1	✹	✹	1		1	✹		1
			1	1		2		✹
	2	✹			✹			✹
1		✹	3	3	✹	4	1		1
✹		✹			✹			1	
✹		1			1		✹	2	
1			3			3	✹		1
	1	✹	✹	✹		2		✹	
		✹		1			2		✹
1	✹	2	1			1	✹		1

Arrow Word (page 106)

Written story	T	Athletics event	T	Person basking	M	Fight	T	Beverage	F	Monk	Desert grains
P	R	O	S	E	Acquires	E	A	R	N	S
Book holding	I	Forearm	U	L	N	A	Longing	I	Withhold	A
S	P	I	N	E	Greek letter	Y	A	R	N
Greek cheese	L	Surpassed	B	E	T	T	E	R	E	D
F	E	T	A	Church song	A	Government tax	N	Plant stalk	S	City in NW France
Obnoxiously forward	J	Hit	T	H	U	D	Pouch	S	E	C
P	U	S	H	Y	Extreme	U	L	T	R	A
Scorn	M	Expel	E	M	I	T	First woman	E	V	E
S	P	U	R	N	Arabian country	Y	E	M	E	N

Split Decisions (page 107)

Answers may vary.

Hitori (page 107)

3	1	8	9	6	6	2
8	9	6	1	6	6	3
1	6	5	8	3	8	6
5	3	6	8	1	1	5
3	5	2	8	8	9	5
6	2	6	5	1	9	8
9	6	3	6	1	2	1

Kakuro (page 108)

		2	9			
	4	1	2			
7	2		7	9	8	
8	1	7		3	1	
		8	9	7		
		2	7			

Spell Math! (page 108)

Five + fifteen = twenty

Red, White, Blue, and Green (page 109)

B	G	R	B	G	W	W	R
B	R	G	R	B	W	W	G
G	R	W	W	R	B	G	B
W	W	B	G	G	R	B	R
W	G	R	W	B	R	B	G
R	B	G	B	W	G	R	W
G	B	W	R	W	G	R	B
R	W	B	G	R	B	G	W

Word Spiral (page 110)

P	O	R	T	R	A	Y	O	N
M	B	O	R	E	E	L	E	D
A	R	E	N	E	M	Y	C	E
J	E	A	S	H	E	T	T	R
G	S	W	E		R	H	R	I
O	N	G	N	I	M	W	I	V
L	E	O	H	T	R	A	C	E
A	T	T	I	M	R	E	H	T
I	D	R	O	C	N	A	R	E

Calcu-doku (page 111)

1	3	4	2
2	1	3	4
3	4	2	1
4	2	1	3

Neighborhood (page 111)

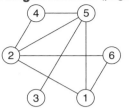

Cross Sums (page 112)

		1316				
	418	408	329			
85	118	161	85	46		
10	9	54	44	37	3	4
12	11	26	1	2		
	5	6	8			
	7					

Mastermind (page 112)

6047

Star Power (page 113)

6	5	4			
7	★	3	8	5	
5	8	1	2	★	1
7	★	3	7	4	6
5	4	2	6	★	5
7	★	1	2	8	1
8	6	3	★	5	
4	7	6			

Chain Sudoku (page 114)

5	1	2	4	3
4	3	1	2	5
1	2	5	3	4
3	5	4	1	2
2	4	3	5	1

Opposites (page 114)

N E A R
F A R

Publishing Poetry (page 115)

Months	Authors	Titles	Editors
August	Dickens	Nine Takes	Valerie
September	Pennington	For Gerald	Marilyn
October	Farnsworth	California	Lyn
November	Beaufort	Driven Away	Jeff
December	Leary	Thieves City	Timothy

Fitting Words (page 116)

```
Y E A S T
O C C U R
W H I N E
L O D G E
```

1-2-3 (page 116)

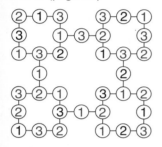

Continuous (page 117)

```
      5 6 2
3   8   4     0
6   4   4     2
1   2   0     3
9   1   9     4
4   1   8     9
0   7   6     1
2   4   3     9
6   1   1     9
4   9   0     9
7   6   3     5
7   0   7     4
2   8   4     6
1   9   5     3
0   7   1     8
0   5   8     8
2   5   9     7
1 9 8   2 1 0
```

Doubled Up (page 118)

The 10-letter word is: Assortment

Starstruck (page 119)

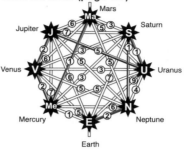

Sequence of letters:

E	N	S	U	J	V	Me	Ma

Days by spacecraft:

2	1	1	5	2	2	1	= 14

Fillomino (page 119)

```
3 1 4 4 4
3 3 4 3 3
2 2 1 3 1
3 3 3 1 3
2 2 1 3 3
```

Domestic Logic (page 120)

Mr. Stark lives in House D.

Word Jigsaw (page 120)

```
T I C
A C U T E
P Y L O N
  L E D
```

Sudoku (page 121)

```
7 9 6 1 2 4 3 5 8
3 1 4 8 7 5 2 6 9
5 2 8 6 9 3 7 1 4
8 6 1 7 4 2 9 3 5
9 4 7 3 5 6 1 8 2
2 3 5 9 1 8 4 7 6
1 7 2 5 8 9 6 4 3
4 5 3 2 6 7 8 9 1
6 8 9 4 3 1 5 2 7
```

Word Sums (page 121)

```
   1 2 5 5
 + 9 4 7 9
 ---------
 1 0 7 3 4
```

Shrouded Summary (page 122)

Struggling young con man murders wealthy friend and assumes his identity, forever fearing discovery. "The Talented Mr. Ripley" by Patricia Highsmith

```
S D N L Y F E R N G J I S T R L O
V T M C O N M A N A S M O E S K L
F R R I U N D U I H E N I T D Y K
W E T U N A L T R H Y C N O M N A
F O E R G V E R E D M U D D V E R
R D E R D G Y O G W E A L T H Y U
D I C S V O L R Y S F R I E N D C
F I D N T H F O L L W S I A N D
N G W R O D S A N N O E T T S H W
O R D W H P P E I G N W H I S O R
D S E H C R N S O I E R O D U I D
U T E O D I V C R O C Y T E M K O
S T R W N K L A N F U S T N E R O
I D P Z L S R A N O I N G T S F R
M I B R N I A W H L B E N I E F T
C O M R P A E N S O S K L T I L D
E W R T I E R C N A B H U Y G E C
O N S E Q E U F O R E V E R N C E
S B A L Y D W O E R D F D L E S R
S E D I S A T S E A R U S O R E M
E M B D I S C O V E R Y B E R R E
A D E R S T P O A T T I E N N O I
T P A R I T U C L R A F N D I E D
A M A G F I N C I D L Q B G C L I
```

Odd-Even Logidoku (page 124)

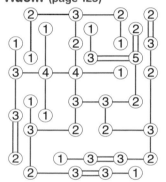

Frame Games™ (page 124)

Banana split

Hashi (page 125)

Chain Grid Fill (page 123)

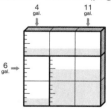

Water Tanks (page 123)

Number Crossword (page 125)

7	8	9	
6	5	4	3
5	5	2	2
	8	5	1

Codeword (page 126)

```
A   W   S       S   T   P
F L O P P Y   S Q U A R E
F   M   E   S   U   X   S
A G A I N S T   E V E N T
B   N   T   O   A   S   S
L I L Y   S C A L P
E   Y   C   K   S   T   G
      C H I R P   B E T A
J   P   I   O   S   D   Z
O L I V E   O U T L I N E
U   X   F   M   U   O
S W I R L S   U N F U R L
T   E   Y       G   S   E
```

1	2	3	4	5	6	7	8	9	10	11	12	13
D	X	Q	R	H	O	M	K	A	P	Z	J	V

14	15	16	17	18	19	20	21	22	23	24	25	26
Y	N	I	S	W	E	L	T	C	B	U	G	F

Times Square (page 127)

1	3	7	7
2	3	1	2
2	1	5	7
2	3	5	1

Word Ladder (page 127)

BRAIN, drain, drawn, drown, frown, FLOWN

Cross Scan (pages 128–129)

1. Wren; 2. dove; 3. kite; 4. rail; 5. sing; 6. soar;
7. flap; 8. eggs; 9. nest; 10. honk; 11. tree;
12. bill; 13. beak; 14. hawk; 15. Bird; 16. raven;
17. eagle; 18. swift; 19. chirp; 20. brood;
21. Wings; 22. perch; 23. grouse; 24. Falcon;
25. gander; 26. Turkey; 27. Martin; 28. cuckoo;
29. flight; 30. cackle; 31. peacock; 32. penguin;
33. flutter; 34. migrate; 35. pigeons; 36. Cardinal;
37. incubate; 38. feathers; 39. Partridge;
40. fledgling; 41. Road Runner; 42. Nightingale
Leftover letters spell: Birds are inventors of
twittering.
Theme: Birds

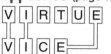

Opposites (page 130)

Arrow Word (page 131)

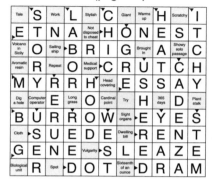

Word Sums (page 131)

$$
\begin{array}{r}
5\ 1\ 3\ 4 \\
+\ 9\ 7\ 4\ 3\ 4 \\
\hline
1\ 0\ 2\ 5\ 6\ 8
\end{array}
$$

Slitherlink Path (page 132)

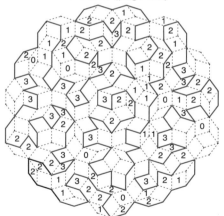

Futoshiki (page 130)

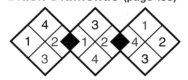

Black Diamonds (page 133)

185

Marbles (page 133)

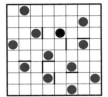

Round and Round (pages 134–135)

G	L	A	M		D	O	R	M		E	F	R	E	M
R	I	T	A		O	R	E	O		R	A	I	M	I
I	M	O	K		G	O	F	O	R	A	S	P	I	N
D	A	Z	E	D			C	O	S	T	A	R	S	
		A	Y	E		C	O	V	E	S				
F	L	O	W	E	R	P	O	W	E	R		C	H	A
J	E	D	I		I	A	N				F	O	I	L
O	R	E	S		C	Y	C	L	E		U	N	D	O
R	O	T	H			O	Y	L		E	D	E	N	
D	I	S		S	L	I	C	E	O	F	L	I	F	E
		D	A	U	N	T		N	A	P				
C	R	U	E	L	L	A			Q	U	A	F	F	
T	O	P	B	I	L	L	I	N	G		M	E	I	R
R	O	D	I	N		I	N	C	A		P	O	L	O
S	M	O	T	E		E	N	O	S		S	N	A	G

Golf (page 136)

Word Jigsaw (page 136)

Mastermind (page 137)

726

Curve Fill (page 137)

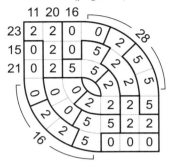

Globe Quest (page 138)

1.	Miami	
2.	New York	42
3.	Chicago	35
4.	Phoenix	39
5.	Denver	54
6.	Atlanta	55
7.	Dallas	36
8.	Los Angeles	38
9.	Seattle	36
	TOTAL	335

Fifteen Up (page 139)

8	5	1	3	7	6	2
7	7	2	8	4	2	11
8	6	2	6	1	1	4
7	3	6	3	2	1	7
6	9	3	2	3	10	2
2	8	7	2	2	5	3
5	5	5	1	5	8	2

Sum Fun (page 139)

2	2	8	4	3	4	2	7	8	7	2
7	5	7	5	9	8	6	3	6	9	1	2
5	2	9	5	9	8	4	3	1	6	8	8
2	6	2	9	8	9	1	5	5	3	4	4
8	5	8	3	3	2	8	3	7	2	9	3
7	8	5	8	5	2	8	7	1	4	7	4
9	8	7	9	7	1	7	4	6	7	8	2
4	6	3	6	7	3	7	7	5	2	7
8	2	8	1	1	6	8	1	6	3	5	8
1	2	8	6	9	7	3	4	7	6	7	7
7	9	6	3	2	4	7	5	3	6	2	7
2	5	7	6	8	9	1	4	7	1	3	2

Animal Rhyme (page 140)

1. mouse/house; 2. crab/cab; 3. mule/fuel;
4. moose/noose; 5. ape/cape; 6. rat/hat;
7. dog/log; 8. goat/boat

Elevator Words (page 141)

1. SQUAWK box; 2. box turtle; 3. turtleneck;
4. neck guard; 5. guard rail; 6. rail fence; 7. fence
SITTER

X and Y (page 141)

There are 7 different values. 1×3, 1×5, 1×7,
3×5, 3×7, 5×7, $0 \times$ any

Klump (page 142)

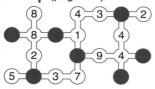

LogiNumber (page 142)

A = 4, B = 3, C = 5, D = 1, E = 2

Star Power (page 143)

		7	4	2			
8	★	1	4	7			
2	5	3	6	★	3	2	6
1	★	4	2	8	5	★	1
8	6	7	★	6	7	4	8
		5	1	3	★	5	
			8	2	1		

Alien Mutations (page 144)

A. remove rear appendages; B. head square;
C. to biped; D. remove antennae; E. add
antennae; F. remove rear appendages; G. body
circle; H. add rear appendages; I. to quadruped;
J. remove front appendages; K. body square;
L. head circle

Grid Fill (page 145)

C	A	M	E	L
F	I	L	E	S
B	O	M	B	S
E	A	R	L	Y
R	E	S	I	N
C	A	V	E	D

Vex-a-Gon (page 145)

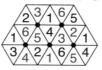

Calcu-doku (page 146)

2	4	1	3	5
5	3	4	2	1
4	5	2	1	3
3	1	5	4	2
1	2	3	5	4

Cross Sums (page 146)

				315				
			100	96	119			
		40	31	29	36	54		
	15	14	11	6	12	18	24	
4	5	6	3	2	1	9	8	7

Indoor Games (page 147)

The leftover letters spell: I like winter because I
can stay indoors without feeling guilty.

187

Spy Fly (page 148)

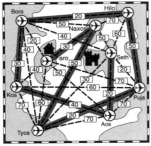

Fillomino (page 148)

4	4	3	3	1
4	4	3	1	3
3	3	1	3	3
3	1	3	4	4
1	3	3	4	4

Codeword (page 149)

S	U	C	K		W	O	N	D	E	R	E	D
E		U		T	X		I		E		E	
L	I	B	E	R	T	Y		S	H	E	A	F
F		E		A		G		H		N		E
I	B	S	E	N		E	J	E	C	T	O	R
M			S		N		A		R		E	
P	A	U	N	C	H		C	R	A	Y	O	N
O		T		E		A		T		T		T
R	E	I	G	N	E	D		E	N	N	U	I
T		L		D		J	N	O		A		A
A	L	I	V	E		U	N	E	Q	U	A	L
N		Z		N	R	N		R		D		L
T	W	E	N	T	I	E	S		E	S	P	Y

1	2	3	4	5	6	7	8	9	10	11	12	13
S	M	F	T	E	V	Q	A	I	R	D	Y	B

14	15	16	17	18	19	20	21	22	23	24	25	26
C	O	L	K	U	W	P	H	Z	J	X	N	G

Split Decisions (page 150)

Answers may vary.

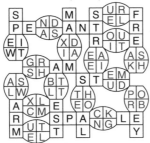

Word Ladder (page 150)

BIGOT, begot, begat, began, vegan, VEGAS

Number Crossword (page 151)

	1	2	3
	4	1	8
4	4	1	
6	4	6	

Battle Boats (page 151)

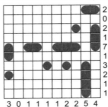

Tanglewords (page 152)

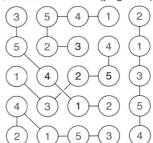

Chain Sudoku (page 153)

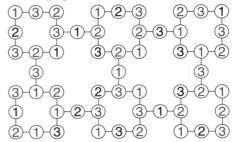

1-2-3 (page 153)

Acrostic (page 154)

"The chains of habit are generally too weak to be felt, until they are too strong to be broken."
A. anthology; B. fly swatter; C. laureate;
D. herringbone; E. notebook; F. Balboa;
G. kitchenette; H. either; I. foots

Kakuro (page 155)

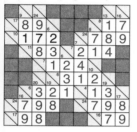

Elevator Words (page 155)

1. WEATHER outlook; 2. Outlook Express;
3. express mail; 4. mail slot; 5. slot racing;
6. racing circuit; 7. circuit BREAKER

Water Tanks (page 156)

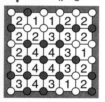

SquarO (page 156)

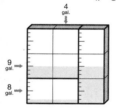

Evens/Odds (page 157)

3	5	1	6	4	2	
1	2		2			
5	4		4	6	2	
4	2	6	1	3	5	4
6			5	4	2	6
2	4	6	3	1	5	

Hitori (page 157)

7	5	9	4	4	3	2	1	8
9	5	7	3	8	6	1	2	1
3	5	8	5	2	7	6	5	1
2	2	1	7	9	9	3	6	
4	6	5	3	3	8	7	1	9
8	9	1	7	6	1	2	6	5
2	3	1	6	5	8	4	4	7
1	7	5	8	3	6	8	2	
2	8	4	8	6	5	5	9	2

Continuous (page 158)

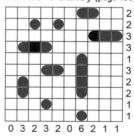

Battle Boats, (page 159)

	2
	2
	3
	3
	1
	3
	2
	2
	1
	1

0 3 2 3 2 0 6 2 1 1

How's Your Recall? (Parts I & II)
(pages 159-160)

Key chain, picture frame, camp tent, opera glasses, treasure chest

L'adder (page 160)

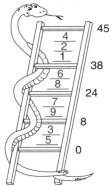

45

$\frac{4}{2}{1}$

38

$\frac{6}{8}$

24

$\frac{7}{9}$

8

$\frac{3}{5}$

0

ABCD (page 161)

B	C	D	C	D	B	A	B	D
A	D	C	A	B	A	B	D	A
D	A	D	B	D	B	D	A	D
B	C	A	C	A	D	C	D	A
A	B	D	A	D	C	D	B	D
C	A	C	D	C	A	C	D	C

Mend the Bridges (page 162)

Answers may vary.

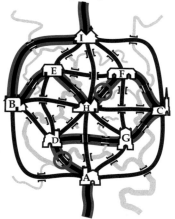

Crypto-Logic (page 162)
REARING

LogiNumber (page 163)
A = 3, B = 4, C = 2, D = 1

Opposites (page 163)

Doubled Up (page 164)
The 10-letter word is: Accidental

XOXO (page 165)

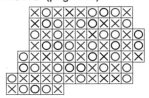

Across the Board (page 165)

6	7	8	9	10	26	27	28	29
5	14	12	11	25	32	31	30	37
15	4	13	24	33	34	35	36	38
16	17	3	23	42	41	40	39	50
18	19	22	2	43	45	48	49	51
20	21	58	57	①	44	46	47	52
60	59	63	78	56	55	54	53	71
61	62	79	64	77	68	69	70	72
⑧⑴	80	65	66	67	76	75	74	73

INDEX